Alandra's Lilacs

Alandra's Lilacs

T R E S S A   B O W E R S

Gallaudet University Press
Washington, D.C.

Gallaudet University Press
Washington, D.C. 20002

© 1999 by Gallaudet University
All rights reserved. Published 1999
Printed in Canada

Library of Congress Cataloging-in-Publication Data

Bowers, Tressa, 1949–
    Alandra's lilacs / by Tressa Bowers.
      p. cm.
    ISBN 1-56368-082-3 (paperback : alk. paper)
    1. Bowers, Tressa, 1949– . 2. Parents of deaf children—United
States Biography. 3. Deaf children—United States—Family
relationships. 4. Parent and child—United States. I. Title.
HQ759.913.B68   1999
649′.1512—dc21   99-23063
                                                 CIP

∞ The paper used in this publication meets the minimum requirements
of American National Standard for Information Sciences—Permanence
of Paper for Printed Library Materials, ANSI Z39.48–1984.

Contents

Preface

Two years ago, my daughter Alandra asked me how I really felt about her deafness. The letter I began to answer her question evolved into this book, as we realized that it might help other parents in our circumstances if they could read about how Alandra's deafness has affected our family. Although at first Alandra was a little hesitant about her life being made so public, she quickly became very enthusiastic about it. She has read every version of this manuscript, liking each one better than the last.

As I wrote, the lyrics to Simon and Garfunkel's hit from years before, "The Sound of Silence," played over and over in my mind:

> *And in the naked light I saw*
> *Ten thousand people, maybe more.*
> *People talking without speaking,*
> *People hearing without listening,*
> *People writing songs that voices never share,*
> *And no one dared*
> *Disturb the sounds of silence.*
> Paul Simon (1964)

This song was a great comfort while I raised Alandra. I was in a time of darkness, lured in by the "neon light" of the oralists and their flashy promises. Each verse of the song described different aspects of my experience with my daughter. Stepping out of that dark land of "cold and damp" and into a world of acceptance was a very long journey. The answer to my quest was hidden for so long, but finally came in the form of sign language. The answer was as obvious as the graffiti we see scrawled everywhere—we see it loudly, boldly, but it only registers as a whisper in our minds. At the end of my road I discovered song in a silent culture, and beauty that voices would never celebrate. As I listen to the song now, I still find new meanings in each verse as I grow in my understanding of the Deaf culture.

I wrote this book to help tear down walls that should never have been built. I also wrote it to let the next generation of parents know the joys, the pitfalls, and the hopes of loving and accepting a deaf child. My husband and I have shared so many of them. Hopefully this book will help hearing parents of deaf children who don't know what to expect, who to listen to, or where to go to ask their questions. I'm not suggesting that I am in any way an authority on what is right for a deaf child. This book is simply a glimpse into our life together, and I'm only suggesting that you follow your heart and love your child. It's the easiest thing in the world to do.

CHAPTER ONE

Reconciliation

The door to my hospital room banged open, startling me awake. I had dozed off. I hadn't wanted to fall asleep but had anyway. My husband Sug (short for Sugar) was next to my bed crying, two nurses stood behind him. In panic, I asked, "What's wrong?" but I already knew what had happened. Sometimes you have a sense of things that are about to go wrong, even when you have never experienced something. You just know. Sug took my hand, gripping it too tightly, and said, "The baby died." I began to cry, sobs racking my body. I curled into a tight ball to stop the empty feeling in the space where my baby had been just six hours before. I could feel the sounds as they burst from somewhere deep inside me—from a place I didn't even know existed. There was a flurry of activity around my bed as the nurses tried to calm me. One of them took my arm, and I felt a needle stick as she gave me a shot to put me to sleep.

I awoke during the night to hear a baby crying down the hall. Reaching for the buzzer I pressed the button to call a nurse. When she entered the room I said, "Please, can someone pick up that poor baby, it's been crying for a long time." The nurse looked at me sadly and said, "There's no baby crying. You've been dreaming, go back to sleep." As she prepared to give me another shot I said, "Of course there is, please go take care of that baby." Just before I blacked out from the shot, the nurse attempted to comfort me: "The only baby in the nursery today was your baby. He didn't live."

When I awoke again I was on a different floor in the main part of the hospital—off the maternity ward. A nurse came in to fill out the forms to register my son's birth and death. When I filled out his name as Lyn Alan, and the nurse gently said, "Mrs. Benjamin, when women lose a baby they often choose a different name so they can keep their favorite name for another baby." I refused. His name had always been Lyn Alan, it couldn't be anything else.

I kept floating in and out of consciousness. I dreamed of my family, although I knew they couldn't come to the hospital.

I was born in Wood River, Illinois in 1949. I had been dating Sug, whose full name was Lyndle Paul Benjamin, Jr., for a while. But when I got pregnant at sixteen, my father and I had a horrible fight. Daddy told me he never wanted to see me again. He instructed my mother that she was not to call me or see me. Even my younger sister and brother were forbidden to see me again.

After getting married, Sug and I went to live with his mother in Pleasant Hill, Illinois, a tiny rural community seventy miles from my hometown. As typical during that time, both towns were segregated—but this was the only thing the two towns had in common. Pleasant Hill's population was only a thousand people, most of them farmers who had known each other all their lives; Wood River was a refinery town, surrounded by heavy industry. Although Pleasant Hill differed greatly from my hometown, I loved the peacefulness of the country.

I was often homesick for my estranged family. We would occasionally sneak in a visit. Mom, Lisa, and Toby drove up once and we were able to spend about an hour together before they had to turn around and go home. It was always a hasty visit but we knew if my father found out there would be hell to pay.

The next time I woke up, Sug and a nurse were standing next to my bed. He was holding my left hand with both of his. Sug was saying something to the nurse, something about taking the baby home to bury. "I want to see my baby," I begged. Sug turned to the nurse and she nodded and left my room. The nurse re-entered carrying a tiny bundle. The body of my baby was wrapped in a rag. It was a receiving blanket that during past uses had been torn in half. I saw my arms as if they were in slow motion, reaching to take the blanket and its contents.

It was incredibly light. I felt a deep cold coming through the folds of the blanket. I gently moved the edges back to reveal its contents, and there was Lyn Alan—all two pounds, two ounces of him. He had black hair and black eyelashes. Examining his hands I found tiny fingers and tinier fingernails. I pulled the rag of a blanket back all the way so I could check him further. He looked so perfect, but his body was cold as I kissed his cheek. The nurse turned her head. Sug began to cry. My heart broke as I gave my baby back to the nurse.

The next time my eyes opened, my mother was standing next to me. I thought I must be dreaming again but she was really there, crying softly. I looked past her and saw my father standing next to my husband. "Daddy!" I cried, holding my arms out to him. For a bright, childish moment, I wanted to go back in time. I wanted this not to have happened. But then my father came to the bed and put his arm around me in a hug. Close to my ear he whispered, "I should have been there for you." It had not been a dream, nothing would change what had happened. Yet here they were, standing in this hospital room eighty miles from their home. Sug had called them after the baby died. Daddy had taken leave (his first ever) from the Alton BoxBoard, the paper mill where he had worked all his life.

He was a hard man, and did not easily forgive those who wronged him. In his mind, I had now been forgiven. The estrangement had ended—but I had had to sacrifice my son. My doctor didn't allow me to go to my baby's funeral, which my father paid for. I harbored anger at my father for the rest of his life. He could accept my baby in death, but could not accept his life. My father never knew of my anger.

CHAPTER TWO

Homecoming

It was the first week of May 1967 when I first brought my daughter home to my mother's kitchen. The whole family, even my maternal grandmother and my great-grandmother, gathered in the kitchen to witness the homecoming. The reunion of five generations of women, all alive and well, was a momentous occasion! It was a wonderful spring day and the breeze entered the room, carrying the smell of lilacs. The huge old bush grew right outside my mother's kitchen window and the perfume of the lilac has always filled the room in the early spring. I have always associated family—in good times and bad—with lilacs, because the kitchen was where my family gathered and spent the day. As I remember those times, my mind smells the wonderful perfume and the memory fills my heart with a longing to share those times with my family once again.

The loss of Lyn Alan the year before had been the most heartbreaking experience I would ever have. Yet life had more or less picked up where it had left off. At seventeen, I was still a child myself. I was naive enough to truly believe love would make everything turn out right. I wanted another baby right away to fill my empty arms. Sug wanted another baby, too. Partly because he wanted to be a husband and father, and partly to avoid the draft.

Before getting pregnant this time, I went to Dr. Frank Morrison, an obstetrician specializing in difficult pregnancies. The prescription he gave me helped me become pregnant within a few months. When he told me I was indeed pregnant, I quickly left his office, eager to tell Sug the good news.

Yet this pregnancy was quite difficult. I had to be confined to bed for weeks because my last baby had been born two months premature. Dr. Morrison told me that all pregnancies were different so I tried to separate the two pregnancies in my mind; yet I constantly feared losing this child. For weeks I lay very still in bed, waiting to feel the first tiny pain signaling my body's betrayal. I was certain I would have a girl. I sometimes allowed myself to dream of a beautiful daughter, only to find myself terrified of losing her. I passed the long hours in my bed alternating between overwhelming fear and sweet dreams, as I waited for my husband to come home. But Sug stayed away as much as he could, probably avoiding fears of his own.

Because of my extreme loneliness and impending due date, I spent the last month of my pregnancy living in my parents' home. My doctor's practice was in a neighboring town, and Sug and I found a house to buy. Daddy even helped get Sug a job at the Alton BoxBoard. I thought everything was going to work out. It was nice being home and getting a little spoiled by all my family.

One night, as the ten o'clock news came on, I went into the living room where my parents were watching TV. I had been to the doctor for a check up just that afternoon.

"Mom, I think maybe I need to go to the hospital," I said. She was settling down to doze in front of the TV, as was her nightly habit. "Are you having labor pains, did your water break?" she asked. I answered no to all her questions. I told her that I felt like I was sitting on an egg, and having contractions but no pain. She laughed, "Well, you're probably having false labor. Why don't you go back to bed, the hospital would just check you and send you home." I agreed and went back to bed. A few minutes later Mother came into my room, where I was trying unsuccessfully to get comfortable. "Daddy thinks I should go ahead and take you to the hospital," she said. I got out of bed and quickly dressed.

During the fifteen-minute drive, I decided I would sure love a root beer float, so Mom and I stopped, bought one each, and brought them with us.

The admitting nurse at the hospital didn't even let me finish answering her questions. She looked at me and said, "Your mother can finish filling out this paperwork, I think we'll go ahead and send you upstairs to be checked." When Mom finished and got upstairs, the nurses were wheeling me out of the delivery room with my baby girl. We named her Alandra, but called her by the nickname Landy.

My daughter was everything I dreamed of. She was the beautiful, tiny baby my arms yearned to hold. She had long black hair and caramel colored skin. Her only resemblance to her Irish heritage was her deep blue eyes and black eyelashes. When I softly tickled her lower lip, her lip puckered and deep dimples appeared in each cheek.

I had just turned eighteen in April and had never been around babies before. Completely lacking any experience, I nevertheless accepted a life-long commitment to this tiny person I held in my arms. On that wonderful spring day when I brought Landy home, my elders were full of well-meaning advice that I eagerly accepted. My daughter was so beautiful and flawless that I wanted to be perfect for her as well. It was a comfort to know that I would have the support and experience of these women through the coming years.

Landy cried that day, and I couldn't figure out why. I had fed and changed her; she was warm without being too warm. I held her close, and everyone laughingly agreed that I would spoil my child for certain. My mother advised, "Sometimes babies just cry to exercise their lungs and you will have to let her cry." My grandmother said, "Maybe she does not like her hands tucked inside the sleeves of her gown." Willing to try anything to make Landy happy, I took her hands with her beautiful long fingers out and she stopped crying.

They told me to put her bassinet in the kitchen so she would get used to noise. Of course I followed their suggestion, although I'm sure it was really because they wanted to look at her and coo like all doting grandmothers—in this case three generations of grandmothers. Again their suggestions were good, and Landy slept soundly and peacefully. She didn't even stir in her tiny bed when we ran the garbage disposal as we cleaned the dishes left from our celebration. My grandmother even commented on that fact: "She is such a calm baby, all this racket isn't even making her flinch."

Three generations of mothers proclaimed her a "good baby," and I, a new mother, was most grateful. It was a good day, full of love, happiness, and hope for the continuity of the family—for there was the living proof that life moves on. All were happy with the celebration and I was pleased to be the one who brought everybody together. The object of our pride and unity was my little daughter, and the scent of that happiness was the lilacs in bloom.

Sug's cousin Denny Motley lived in a nearby town. His wife Linda was older than me, and an elementary school teacher. I had dropped out of high school after getting pregnant, so I had a lot of respect for her education. We became good friends and like many couples with little money, spent a lot of time visiting in each other's homes. Their daughter, Joy, was about two years old and had been born deaf. (During her pregnancy, Linda had been exposed to the measles, the three-day kind that everyone used to get. I was surprised that a childhood disease that didn't even make you very sick could cause something so severe.) I had never been around a child with a hearing problem, but Linda was always glad to answer my questions and taught me to talk with Joy. It was very important to talk to her on her level so she could see your mouth and learn to read lips, or speechread. So we spent most of our time—for as long as we could hold their attention anyway—sitting on the floor playing with Joy and Landy. After the kids went to sleep Linda and I played cards or just talked, sharing ideas and enjoying our time together.

Joy wore a hearing aid called a body aid. It was a bulky box of a thing, which she wore in a harness around her chest. A cord traveled up from the box to a large button-like component in her ear. She could hear really well with it and her speech developed at a good pace. Whenever she was not wearing her hearing aid, she would run through the house screaming and laughing wildly. You had to laugh at her antics because she was enjoying herself so much; yet although I enjoyed visiting, I was sure happy to take my ringing ears and go home. I soon understood that Joy was just trying to hear herself. Like people who begin to talk louder and louder as they lose their hearing, Joy didn't realize how loud she was. When she wore her hearing aids, her voice was much more controlled and life was a lot easier on the hearing people around her.

Like any little girl, Joy wanted to hold my daughter and play with the live baby doll. The two girls looked like exact opposites: Joy was blonde and fair (she looked like a Dresden doll) and Landy had almost-black hair and a light olive complexion. When they played side by side, you were immediately struck by not only their differences, but by their beauty. Joy spent many weekend days playing sweetly with Landy. The play times they shared may have been the only time Joy ever approached a state of calm during her terrible twos.

When Landy was around five months old, I started to suspect that she was also deaf. I don't even remember what made me suspicious. But fear, like a cancerous worm, began intruding into my happiness. During the early part of my pregnancy I knew I had been exposed to the three-day measles while babysitting for my husband's nieces and nephew. There had been a measles epidemic and all the kids were getting them. The kids had not been feeling well, so I wasn't surprised when they broke out in a rash from head to toe. The next day I called my obstetrician, who asked if I had ever had the measles before. I replied, "Yes, several times." He said, "Well, the current thinking in the medical field is that a person can only get the three-day measles once, so your baby will not be at risk." I said, "Once! I have had them more than once. I know you can get them again." My doctor said, "Well, since you can only have measles once, you can't get the gamma globulin shot. But don't worry about the baby, it will be fine." So I put the thoughts and the worries out of my head. But the fears always had a way of returning, regardless of the comforting advice I received.

I tentatively broached the subject of my fears while visiting Linda and Joy one afternoon. "Linda," I said, "I think sometimes that Landy is deaf." Laughing, she replied, "From time to time all kids pretend they don't hear you." Shaking my head, I said, "No, it's more than that. I *really* don't think she hears." Linda gave my remark a little more consideration, but then said, "I'm sure you're wrong, it's just your imagination playing tricks on you. It's because you're around Joy so much." Then carefully selecting her words so not to hurt my feelings, she added, "And partly it may be because you lost the first baby." Giving in, I agreed she was probably right.

Voicing my suspicions for the first time relieved my fears for a while. Yet there were so many little things that I kept noticing—similarities to Joy, differences from my other nieces and nephews. I just couldn't shake the memory of keeping the kids the day they broke out with the measles. A few weeks later Landy and I visited her pediatrician. Not only had Dr. Buzan been practicing pediatric medicine for many years, he had seven children of his own. If anyone would know if my daughter were deaf, he would be the one. I told him about my fears. When I told him I had been exposed to the measles during my pregnancy, he suddenly grew more alert. But he relaxed when I told him I had the measles as a child. Like Linda, he thought it was my imagination and new mother jitters. In fact, his remarks were almost identical to hers: "Because you lost the first baby, perhaps you are looking for something to be wrong with this one." When I assured him this was not the case, he said, "The best thing to do is to take her home and enjoy her. If you still think she can not hear when she's a year old, you'll need to take her to an ear, nose, and throat doctor."

I felt frustrated that he brushed my fears aside so lightly. I was sure he was laughing at me because I was so young. My anger flaring, I thought, I certainly do enjoy my baby. What does he think I want, a refund? But I did not speak these thoughts out loud. After all, he was the doctor. I felt frustrated because these experts were unable to see what was so obvious. I was embarrassed, angry with myself because they made me feel so inept at being a mother. I began keeping my fears to myself so people couldn't laugh or make me feel inadequate. My "experts" had refused to see, refused to look, refused to listen.

Months passed and I tested Landy using my own less-than-scientific methods. I unwrapped candy behind her back—when she turned around immediately, I cursed myself for being a fool and getting worked up over nothing.

But when moments later I would call her and get no response, I told myself, I know she is deaf. I was on an emotional rollercoaster. I shared my feelings with no one except my beautiful baby. I held her and told her about all of my worries; she responded by sweetly smiling and cooing. Much later I realized that Landy was feeling my step on the floor, and smelling the candy even before I opened it all the way.

We finally went back to the pediatrician for Landy's one-year check up. I was pregnant again and thought this fact alone should give me more credibility as a mother. It may have been overactive hormones, but this time I was armed with a grim determination to be taken seriously. I started our visit by saying firmly, "Doctor, I still do not think my daughter can hear." Dr. Buzan was a kind man and a very gentle doctor; my obvious distress did not put him off. He questioned me about why I still thought she was deaf, so I described all the ways I had been testing her. Finally he admitted, "I really can't tell if she's able to hear or not, there wasn't very much training in medical school for this kind of problem." I let out the breath I had been holding, my distress easing. Finally, we were finally discussing the issue! He said, "You need to make an appointment with an ear, nose, and throat doctor and have her hearing checked by a specialist." I thanked him for his honesty, and mentally I gave a sigh of relief—someone was listening! Now at least I might get my questions answered. Feeling better, when I took Landy home that day I felt more relaxed than I had in months.

I looked in the phone book, but it listed very few local doctors specializing in ear, nose, and throat. My daughter and I had to wait months for an appointment. During the wait, I found little relief. I was unable to share my concerns with my husband; he spent little time at home. Sug said he was going "night fishing" but of course he never brought home any fish. Of course I knew the truth—I was just reluctant to voice it. I guess that I had always known that our marriage had been one of convenience; I wanted someone of my own to love me and Sug wanted to avoid Vietnam. Yet I was pregnant, had dropped out of school, and our daughter might be deaf. What was I going to do, get a divorce?

Even my mother and her wonderful kitchen with the lilac bush brought me little joy that summer. Our visits and conversations were lectures on sticking out a bad marriage, not about whether Landy could hear. My parents seemed reluctant to even consider the possibility of Landy's deafness.

One day that summer my mother and I visited my paternal grandparents. They were both warm, loving, and generous people and I wondered if their feelings for Landy would change once we got a diagnosis. Grandma Loraine took in laundry and her kitchen always smelled like freshly ironed shirts. Catching her up on the latest news, I said, "I'm taking Landy to see a specialist. I don't think she can hear." Grandma looked up from the shirt she was working on and said, "Don't tell Grandpa, it will just kill him. He just loves all the babies so much." I had expected to make explanations to other people, outsiders, about my daughter's deafness—but had not expected it from my own family. I decided right then that this was not another little family secret to be swept under the rug.

Getting up from my place at the table, I walked right in to my Grandpa's TV room. He was bouncing Landy on his knee and loudly singing "Ride A Cock Horse." (Grandpa Van Hoy was a bit hard of hearing himself.) When he saw me, he stopped singing and gave me his usual big smile. "Grandpa," I said, "I wanted you to know that we think Landy is deaf." He gave Landy a big hug and boomed, "Well, I wondered why she didn't pay attention to me when I talked to her!" Then he started bouncing her up and down again, singing even louder than usual. As it turned out, he was one of the more accepting people in the family.

A month after our visit to the pediatrician, I gave birth to my second son a month early. Although the nurses and doctors were pretty optimistic about his chances of survival, I was not. I felt like I was going into that delivery room not to give life, but to bring death. Lyndle Paul, III, weighed only four-and-a-half pounds when he was born. Even his name was bigger than he was. I had named him after his father and grandfather, who had died when Sug was just ten years old. I was going to call him Lyn, after my first son. But my tiny baby began to have breathing difficulties immediately after his birth. Looking tired and sad, Dr. Buzan came in to my room and said, "Mrs. Benjamin, your baby will probably not live though the night." I nodded through the fog of the anesthetic I had been given during delivery.

Two days later the baby gave up fighting for his life. He would be my last child and in my mind, his would be the hand that always encouraged me to be a better mother to my only living child. I have always kept the two boys close to me in my heart and mind, and each time I kiss my daughter, I kiss all three of my children. Perhaps I lost the other children so I would be able to better devote myself to the challenges ahead. I didn't grieve so badly this time, but I held my daughter closer, fearful that I would lose her too.

Still recovering from the birth and passing of my son, I dressed Landy in her prettiest dress and little patent leather shoes, as though the way she was dressed would make a difference in the outcome. My stomach was in a knot during the fifteen-minute drive. I knew what the doctor was going to say, but still I prayed he would tell me I was wrong. As I walked into the doctor's building I held my baby closer. I fought the urge to stop and go back to the car, to take Landy home before the doctor could proclaim that she was deaf. I didn't want to hear the diagnosis, but I had to know! I kissed her little ears, remembering that when I was pregnant I had prayed she would have pretty ears (not her father's ears, which I felt were too big). I cursed myself because I had forgotten to pray that her pretty ears would work.

Dr. Bly was an older man and I am sure he was very wise for his day. After we talked of my concerns he put all his training to work. He had me hold Alandra on my lap and get her attention. He walked behind me and dropped a metal pan on the floor, then came back around to face me. Sitting down on a stool, the doctor picked up a heavy metal instrument that he called a tuning fork. It looked like a heavy metal Y, like if you drew the Y in a square method instead of the pointed method we were taught in grade school. Striking it, Dr. Bly placed the long end of the Y behind my daughter's ear; she did not react. As he took it away he declared, "She's stone deaf." The good doctor (with all of his gracious bedside manner) then said, "Your baby most likely will never be able to talk, and probably will not get much education because of the limitations of communication." He went on to say, "She will probably make a lot of 'different' sounds. Someday she will probably make sounds in public that will embarrass you."

I have never told Alandra about the doctor's harsh words, keeping them a darkly hidden secret. I never wanted my daughter to think that I could ever be anything but proud of her. I still wonder how a doctor specializing in hearing problems could ever think such cruel thoughts, let alone repeat them to a parent. I have learned over the years that many people—even doctors—can be cruel with the things that they say. Today, I am quick to correct them for their ignorance and bad manners. But when I was nineteen, doctors and their education awed me; Bly's words cut me deeply. The doctor's final words were, "The condition is known as 'nerve deafness' and there isn't a way to correct it medically." This ended our one and only appointment. I thanked the doctor for his time, paid the bill, and left with my mind in a fog.

I was angry with the doctor—not for his confirmation of deafness nor his lack of compassion—but for the insensitive way in which he had given me the news. I was angry with God for making innocent little babies deaf, and for not giving the doctors the knowledge to correct it. I felt God had made something so perfect when He made Landy, and then He looked at her and decided to take something away.

Yet I didn't feel as though my world had fallen in on top of me. Landy was perfectly normal in every other way, and she was a beautiful baby. I had felt tragedy before, with the loss of my two sons. I told myself that deafness, at least, can be dealt with. Although it was painful, it was not tragic. I knew that my life was going to be forever different, but somewhere deep inside I felt a tingle of excitement for that difference.

Now that I knew for sure, I had lots of things to do. My experience with Linda and Joy had taught me that nothing could be done to correct the problem, but that Joy could talk—so of course Landy would talk. As far as the educational aspect, I would prove the doctor wrong on that accord as well. I would teach her myself if necessary. Landy was only a year old but I could tell she was bright; I just needed to find the way to unlock all that intelligence.

That night I did two things. First, I called my friend Linda and told her the news. She gave me the phone number for the state's Crippled Children's Foundation, a non-profit organization that provided financial aid and other types of support to children with disabilities. Later, after I got Landy down to bed, I indulged in a good cry. Sug and I were sitting in our living room, staring silently at the TV. As usual, I received little or no consolation from my husband. He had become a cardboard figure in my life, only there when it suited him. Glaring at me, he said, "I don't understand why you're crying, we already knew that she was deaf." I ignored him. Through those tears I cried out the grief and the stress I had been feeling those many months when I spoke to no one about my fears. I cried for Landy and I cried for me. I cried for two little boys who would never know my love. I cried for a marriage that was not what I dreamed of and I cried for a God who would turn His back on those I loved.

But that would be the only time I would give in to tears of pity and worry. As Paul Simon sang, I "turned my collar to the cold and damp." Although there were tough times ahead, I resolved that any crying from then on would be tears of joy from our many successes. I would receive little support from my husband. I realized that evening that whatever my child's future would be, it would have to be of my making.

The Race Begins

During the next few weeks I put aside my worries and got right to work. As I tried to find information about deafness, financial help, and education, Linda became my best resource. She told me that every day a deaf child goes without education is like three days for a hearing child. That was such a frightening thought, but it had the desired effect and I began a race against time. All parents are concerned about their children's future—hearing parents of deaf children just have to start worrying sooner. The educators and the doctors make you feel that there are deadlines to be met, constantly reminding you of all the other deafness-related factors you need to think about. I worried that lacking a formal education, I would not know the best form of education for my deaf daughter. I was faced by the challenge of two handicaps: Landy's was physical, mine was educational.

My husband's pay was about $150 every two weeks and hearing aids were expensive. Because we were considered a low-income family, we were entitled to financial aid. I applied to many charitable organizations for help, and finally heard from the Crippled Children's Foundation. Linda had taken Joy through this program and told me they were very thorough. They set up hearing tests at two hospital clinics in St. Louis, Missouri. The testing showed a 95-decibel loss in both ears and no hearing at all in the speech ranges. Although the foundation helped us purchase a hearing aid, their doctors assured me that there was no medical treatment for this type of deafness. Oddly though, later testing showed that Landy has what the doctors call residual hearing in the frequency of things as soft as a kiss, if the sound is made up close to her ear. To this day my daughter hates that sound, so we never do it, but I do think it is interesting that someone who can not hear you shout her name can hear something as quiet as a kiss.

I learned to understand the charts and graphs of the hearing tests. I learned to understand the language doctors used to describe Landy's hearing loss. I also learned that the loss was not just one of loudness but of clarity; just making the sounds louder would not help her hear them. Still, I thought that a hearing aid would solve many of her everyday hearing problems. I did not understand, nor was I told of, the different points of view regarding language acquisition. The oralists are quick on the scene when a child is diagnosed as deaf. The doctors at both hospitals advised me in the oralists' direction. When I found out a few years later that there was another way to learn language, I firmly believed in the oral method.

Early on, the people I met wanted to correct the problem and to make Landy as close to "hearing" as possible. I patiently listened to every suggestion, no matter how outrageous; one person thought we should have Landy "healed" at a tent revival. But there was a wonderful gentleman with the Shriner fraternal organization. He contacted us, saying he wanted to sponsor Landy with a Shriner hospital that could give her an operation to correct her hearing loss. In my heart I wished for a cure, but I told him, "We have been told that she has nerve deafness and there is no way to correct the problem." He reassured me that the Shriners have access to the world's best doctors and of course they could correct the problem. He said, "As Landy's sponsor, I will take her to the big Christmas party every year and I will always follow her life and be part of it." He was so positive and so hopeful—how could I refuse? We agreed that he would present her case at their next meeting.

After presenting the case to the medical board, the doctors confirmed what I had told him. Because the nerve that changes the sound waves to electrical impulses was damaged or just not there, there was nothing they could do to correct Landy's deafness. I think he was more hurt than I. There were tears in his eyes when he told me her case was rejected, and I found myself consoling him. I asked, "Did you know that Spencer Tracy's son is deaf and so he founded a school and clinic in California? I have been in contact with the clinic and they have sent me a lot of very good information on early education and communication." I'm so very sorry to have forgotten the gentleman's name, but I have never forgotten how touched I was by his concern for my daughter or the wonderful things the Shriners do for so many children. I hope he found a child who could be helped in some other way.

I was having trouble finding a school for Landy. Apparently, the state's education programs didn't accept students younger than three. During a family gathering at my parent's house I cornered my uncle, who happened to be a state school superintendent. My father's brother, Dr. Clarence Van Hoy, Jr., was the educational success of our blue-collar family, working hard for one degree after another. If anyone could point me in the right direction, I knew it would be him. I asked him why there was no education available locally for deaf children. Putting on his business persona, my uncle replied, "Deafness is a low-incident need and it is very expensive to meet the needs of the few. It is more cost effective to hire the best teachers the state can, locate them in one school—in this case we have a boarding school in Jacksonville—and then bring the students to the teachers. In other words," he continued, "in a town like ours, there may only be one or two deaf students and that is too few to create a program for."

Fidgeting under the family's silent gaze, he said, "It is always hard to tell a parent something like this." I was sure it was even harder when that person was your niece, and I felt sorry for him. Still, if I had listened better, I would have learned much sooner about sign language and other education possibilities. Boarding school? No way! He affirmed Linda's advice about the parent/infant programs available in St. Louis and advised me on asking our state Department of Education for financial help.

I don't remember much about the process after that, except that there were pages and pages of forms. I filled them out the best I could, but the huge stack of forms and documents was overwhelming. Some of the forms were financial; those were tough because I was not involved with our financial responsibilities. Others had to be filled out by doctors. I had to wade through all of them. I'm sure it would be an expensive service, but it would have been a great deal of help if I could have hired someone to fill out the paper-work. It took several weeks to finish because I was working alone and didn't understand most of the questions. Some days I just couldn't bear to pick up the pile and concentrate. I began to panic about all the time passing. Finally I had the papers as complete as possible, and mailed them back.

Weeks passed without hearing anything in return. I had inherited my father's lack of patience. A few days would pass and I would think of the time that was being wasted. At first I panicked, then became angry that there was no way to speed up the process. One evening, I decided to call Governor Samuel H. Shapiro at home. Pretending to be a friend, I asked for Sam. After a brief wait, the man who originally answered came back on the line and asked me what the call was in reference to. Caught! After telling him that my infant daughter was deaf and we needed help paying for school, I was cordially invited to call Governor Shapiro at the office. A few days later I received a letter from the Department of Education giving me financial aid to en-roll Landy in the Central Institute for the Deaf (CID). I was certainly impressed with what you could get done when you had the right connections.

The process of applying for financial assistance, having more precise hearing tests, and waiting for the hearing aid to be designed to meet Landy's needs took several months. Lilac season was past, and fall 1968 was upon us. Landy was almost a year-and-a-half old when the hearing aid supplier called to tell me the hearing aid was ready.

We rode the bus to Alton to pick up her hearing aid. I was excited, but Landy had no idea what we were doing. I tried to explain, but Landy had no way to understand what I was saying. She enjoyed the trip anyway, because she had never been on a bus before. When we finally got to the hearing aid store, they showed me how to put it on her and told me the first time should be in a quiet environment. She should wear it for about thirty minutes and build up to wearing it all day.

While we waited at the bus stop outside the hearing aid supplier's shop, an elderly lady began cooing at my beautiful daughter. I didn't want this woman to think I was raising the child to be impolite, so when Landy didn't respond I patiently explained that my daughter was deaf and could not hear her. I was not ready for the woman's response: "You must be very wicked to have received such a punishment from God." I couldn't believe someone could be so spiteful! I was only nineteen years old, and vulnerable to people and their cruelties. I stood on the street corner with my beautiful baby in my arms, looking for any reason why someone would use their God as a weapon against somebody else. How could she claim that a parent's wickedness caused this extreme wrath on an innocent child? She must be certifiably crazy, I thought, a sane person wouldn't even think something like that, let alone say it. Near tears and completely deflated, I forgot all my mother's words about respecting your elders. I told her to "just get away from me, you stupid old fool." What I really wanted to do was punch her, scream at her, so that all my anger, hurt, and frustration could pour out of me and into that nasty old woman.

The woman's harsh words turned me from all religious

comfort. I felt God had turned His back on my child and the many others like her. From that day on, I put my faith in science. Science seemed the one field that recognized the limitations of knowledge and humanity's inability to prevent some things from happening. My very logical mind embraced science for accepting the responsibility for my daughter's deafness.

Wounded and hurt, but mostly angry, I took my daughter to my mother's kitchen for her first experience with her hearing aid. I consoled myself with the knowledge that my daughter would never have to hear that kind of ignorance from people.

CHAPTER FOUR

The Sounds of Silence

Sitting at the kitchen table I told my mother about my encounter with the crazy woman at the bus stop. She didn't know how to make me feel better, but agreed that at least Landy wouldn't have to listen to such ignorant people. Then she advised me to ignore people who said things to purposefully hurt me. That was not exactly the kind of advice I cared to hear (but it would prove helpful later during an encounter with my maternal grandmother). I know now that my anger actually helped me through the hard years that followed.

My mother and I put Landy's hearing aid on her and sat her on the kitchen table. We turned it on and were both silent for a moment, then I said "hello." Landy's eyes grew wide. Seeing her reaction, tears spilled from my mother's eyes and mine. What a joy to see the smile and that wonderful light that came over my daughter's face the very first time she heard my voice. She could really hear! Wicked old women and their thoughtless tongues could no longer hurt me on this day. I had attained heaven!

Landy didn't seem to mind wearing the hearing aid, so in my excitement I forgot to remove it. Every day after that, I left the hearing aid on her for the entire day. I began my testing again. What could Landy hear with her hearing aid and what could she hear without it? Mother and I made sounds by clapping our hands and stomping our feet just to see her turn around and smile. Her other senses were so keen, though, that it was difficult to tell what she was really hearing. Often when we thought she was hearing a sound, she was actually feeling vibrations, using her peripheral vision, or smelling something with that little button nose. We nevertheless persisted in the testing, and it became a game. However, other experiences were not as much fun.

My maternal grandmother often asked me to bring Landy to her house more often. Her name was Bertie Isbell, but when I was a child she called me a pickle puss. I teased her back by calling her Picky Puss, and the name stuck. It was a good fit, Grandma Picky Puss was just not a very nice person. Although she said she wanted to know all of her great-grandchildren, I had procrastinated. Now, though, Landy had a new hearing aid and I wanted to share my joy with everyone in the family. Soon after getting Landy's hearing aid I took her for a visit, wanting Grandma to see how hopeful things were now that Landy could hear so much better.

We hadn't been at Grandma's home very long and she hadn't even offered us anything to eat. Sitting at the table in her kitchen, I noticed how unusually quiet she was. Gazing out the window, she finally said, "Tressa, I don't want you to bring your baby back here anymore. It just bothers me too much that she can't hear." Stunned, I stared at her in disbelief. Still sitting quietly, she told me, "The little girl across the street is retarded. She just sits and swings all day.

I sit here at the table and watch her and think of your poor little baby. I don't want you to bring her anymore, I just can't stand it." Picking up my daughter and walking towards the door, I said, "Okay Grandma—it will be your loss, not hers. She will never know you existed."

We never went back to my grandmother's house, and I never called her on the phone. I didn't miss her, but it hurt that she could reject my daughter so easily. I comforted myself with the knowledge that she had never been a very loving grandmother to any of her grandchildren. As a child I was never even offered a cookie at her house; if I asked for one, I was told they were for my grandfather's lunch. No, my daughter would not miss much. I was very careful not to run into her at my mother's house and to my knowledge, Grandma never asked about us. The rejection didn't hurt Landy because she never knew her great-grandmother. The day Grandma Picky Puss died I couldn't even pay my condolences to my mother. I had succeeded in cutting her out of my life completely.

Alandra loved to get her bath in the evenings; but even more than that, she loved to scream while in the bathtub. We had a huge old-fashioned tub, the kind with claw feet. Bathrooms have the best acoustics, but when you slide down deep into a claw-foot tub, the sound just vibrates around you. The tub was so deep the rim was over Landy's head when she was sitting down. Landy would give a shrill scream, pretending to be frightened, and in response I would let out a high-pitched scream of my own. I needed to let off steam to keep my sanity and besides, I told myself, Landy might learn to respond to sound. With all of the porcelain surrounding us, the sounds bounced everywhere— including inside my head long after we stopped.

Landy often put on long shows for the family after she finished her bath and was dressed so sweetly in her night-gown. She was very animated, almost like a mime (this was probably her own form of early sign language). She twirled and danced and even took her bows, while we laughed and clapped like this was truly the greatest show on earth. We played games for everything, animating or miming different events, but never used sign language. At night I lay down with her to get her to sleep, and I quietly stroked her face and her forehead in the absence of stories or songs.

It was about 1969 when my parents bought their first color television. Landy was two years old, and she loved it. She enjoyed TV, even though we knew she could not hear what was being said. We surmised that she understood most of what was going on just by watching—this was long before the days of closed captioning. The day after Landy and I visited my parents to admire their new TV, she seemed angry with our TV at home and kept marking up the screen with her crayons. I had to clean the screen several times a day. After a few days of this, I realized that she thought she could make our TV into a color set by coloring the screen. With restraint I finally left Landy's crayon marks on the screen for a week. I guess she understood that coloring the TV would never make it a color set, because she finally stopped doing it.

Sometimes it took a while to understand what Landy was trying to communicate, and I just had to keep digging. I began to develop a sense of humor regarding the differences between my child and a hearing child. These were the traits that helped make her a precious, unique individual. This awareness was also the beginning of my acceptance of her differences, and my introduction to the beautiful world she was leading me into.

Central Institute for the Deaf in St. Louis had a parent/infant program—and thanks to my good friend, the governor, we were enrolled in the class. I drove to the school once a week for an hour-long class that taught me how to work with my daughter at home. CID was located about thirty miles from our home and deep in the heart of the city—not far from the large hospital complex where I had taken Landy for testing. I was nineteen years old by then, but I had never driven outside my own surrounding area of about four small towns. The drive took about an hour, taking me down Kingshighway Boulevard, past long stretches of shops with iron bars covering every window and door.

The program at CID was strictly oral. In other words, no signing or gesturing was allowed—not by parents or students. The school's philosophy was that although it takes many hours of seeing speech on the lips, a deaf child could learn to speak and integrate successfully into the hearing world. The teachers told me any signing would become a crutch and would slow our efforts to make my child speak. The school made every effort to place my daughter's success or failure directly on my shoulders.

The teachers at CID convinced me that my daughter could be oral, and I readily agreed. A hearing child, they told me, had to hear a word thousands of times before she could say it herself. A deaf child, however, needed to see the words many thousand times more before she could mimic the movement and the sound. It would be a very long process indeed. I eagerly embraced their methods so that my beautiful baby could be normal.

Pointing was forbidden, but I could cast my eyes in the direction of the object I was talking about. We worked so hard for the next two years! When Landy could finally say a few words, "ball" sounded like "baaw" and "more please" sounded like "mo peas." Yet we were making good progress and she was speechreading even more than she could say at the end of our two years at CID. Oddly, my hands never wanted to be completely still. Our teacher repeatedly scolded me for trying to assist my daughter's understanding by pointing. When the teacher finally told me that both my daughter and I could be expelled from the program, I bristled. I began to doubt the school's commitment to teaching deaf children. It seemed that if they truly wanted to communicate with their students, they would not put such constraints on the means with which to do so. However, I knew no other way. I had only a vague concept of sign language, so I complied with the school's demands.

There were some things about CID that were truly fun, however. During the time Landy and I were students at CID, our teacher asked us to help film a training video. They wanted a segment showing Landy and me making cookies in the kitchen, communicating using the oral techniques we had learned at the school. They showed the video to prospective students and their parents, as well as adults who were studying at CID to become teachers. Years later, I actually met a woman who had seen the video!

During the summer that Landy was two years old, the Illinois School for the Deaf in Jacksonville put on a seminar for the parents of young deaf children. I never knew how we got on the list of families to be invited, but I was anxious to attend. The same evening I received the invitation to the two-week program, I showed it to my husband and asked him if we could go. Sug said he couldn't get off work, but I could go alone if I wanted. I immediately returned my acceptance form.

The Illinois School for the Deaf was a "live in," or residential, school, and Landy and I stayed in the dorms that students lived in during the school year. Linda and Joy were also invited, so we were together much of the time and were able to discuss the things we learned. While our children were in day care, we went to classes to learn what to expect in the years to come.

I specifically remember one psychologist who spoke to the parents during an assembly one evening. He was deaf and spoke very well, but I thought he sounded as if he had a slight foreign accent. He told us that we needed to learn sign language. He said that if we were not able to communicate well with our children they might reject us as they grew older—especially in the teenage years—because they would learn sign language from one another even if they were taught by the oral method.

I immediately put that out of my mind because CID said my daughter would be able to talk—and they were the best available minds on the subject. After all, here was this very successful deaf man using his almost perfect voice to tell us how important it was to learn sign language to communicate with our children. It was almost a contradiction. I was rather shy and insecure at that time of my life. Using sign language would get people's attention; they might even stare at us. I would not have people staring at my daughter, and resolved that she would learn to talk just like normal people. (Today, I tell my daughter, "Don't worry about it," when people stare as we use sign language. I tell her they are just naturally curious and many are as fascinated as I myself am.)

I thought to myself, Of course Landy will be able to talk. It will just take longer than with most children, but we certainly will not have a communication problem. And since she will never attend a school that uses sign language, she will never be exposed to it in the first place.

While I completely ignored what the psychologist had to say about sign language, I learned a lot of other things from his lecture. He told us that almost everybody in our children's circle of friends would be deaf, that it might be difficult to speechread another deaf person, and that usually Deaf people marry within the Deaf community. One of the parents raised his hand to ask, "Why do you say that Deaf people usually marry other Deaf people?" After a sign language interpreter translated the question, the psychologist replied, "A deaf person's voice does not sound the same as a hearing person's voice. It is not very romantic to listen to the words 'I love you' uttered by a deaf lover at that very special moment." Even though this man spoke very well and was very articulate, I had to agree his voice was different. I tried to imagine myself in a romantic moment with a deaf man. I thought the sound of his voice would not be a problem, but didn't like the thought of him not hearing me whisper the words back.

The psychologist also told us that most children born to deaf couples could hear, unless the parents' deafness was an inherited trait. I don't know why, but that certainly sank in. I felt in my heart what he said was true, so I always believed Landy would marry a deaf man, her friends would be deaf, and her children would be hearing. In my mind it was such a rosy picture, everyone talking, everyone being quite "normal." I took everything that man said as fact—except the need for sign language. Was I not listening? Or was I just too naive to believe?

During the two-week program at the Illinois School for the Deaf, the parents passed around a horror story by word of mouth. There was probably little or no truth to the story, and I retell it now not to frighten but only to show to readers who do not have deaf children how frightening some aspects of raising a deaf child can be. As parents we each have our own fears and deal with them as best we can. This was one of my fears, one that still haunts me in my nightmares.

According to the story, a deaf boy and his mother were shopping in a large St. Louis department store one Saturday. They somehow got separated, and after a long search of the store he was not found. Finally the officials decided that the boy was no longer in the store and abandoned the search. Stores in St. Louis were not open on Sunday, but on Monday morning the boy was found in the store—alive, but terrified. He had been stuck in an elevator. Unable to call for help or hear anyone calling, he had remained trapped in the elevator over the weekend.

My heart would skip beats in panic when we were shopping and Landy left my sight. She was so independent, so fearless, she would pull away from me and walk off. This independence later proved to be one of her strengths, but remembering it still makes my blood turn cold. I still have nightmares about the possibility of this kind of thing happening; but in my dreams my daughter has been replaced with two little boys, and I am madly searching, racing against time before they are lost forever. Today I don't shop very often.

I was always afraid of the potential for danger in our surroundings. Our neighborhood was in a typical small town, but our home was only two blocks from a main thoroughfare and the local high school. It was not unusual for teenagers to speed up and down our street. We spent a lot of time at my parent's home on Sixth Street, which linked two busy state highways. On one side of Sixth Street were houses, on the other side was an oil refinery surrounded by a chain link fence. Oil tankers traveled this road from one refinery to another; the air was always filled with dust because their tires would edge off the pavement onto the side of the road. Although I was very watchful, I knew I could not hold Landy's hand her whole life. One of my solutions was to take Landy up and down both streets, introducing her to the neighbors. I carefully explained that if she were in front of a driveway, she would not hear a car horn honk to let her know she should get out of the way. My technique may have been overcautious, but it worked. My smallest cry of alarm would send all of our neighbors rushing out to help find her. I tried to protect her from all the possible "what ifs" I could imagine; and maybe because nothing bad ever happened, she grew more independent and more fearless every day.

CHAPTER FIVE

Total Communication

The state of Illinois provided education for deaf children beginning at the age of three, so after Landy's birthday in 1970 the state stopped paying for her to attend CID, which was in Missouri. Now Sug and I had a choice to make.

We were already familiar with the Illinois School for the Deaf in Jacksonville. It was seventy miles away, so Landy would have to live in a dorm. Also, the school taught sign language. The other option was the new local program for hearing-impaired students. The program was in a public school in South Roxanna, just a few miles from our home, and it used oralism and lip-reading. There really was only one choice. I couldn't bear the thought of leaving my three-year-old daughter in the care of a residential school. I was also convinced that in some instances the oral method is very successful, and I held on to the hope that Landy would be one of those successes.

So every morning I put my three-year-old on the school bus that took her to the local program. She looked so small and cute carrying her lunch box up the steps into the bus. Her work continued at home—speechreading, speech, all the things I felt compelled to teach my daughter. I worked with Landy hour after hour. Still, our strictly oral method was very constricting, and trying to communicate was often very frustrating. Landy could say about forty different words and I was proud of every one of them, knowing how hard we had worked to achieve them.

However, forty words certainly did not give her enough language to really communicate. As an infant it was easy to guess what she needed, but as she grew older Landy developed wants and needs that she had no way to communicate. But the educators had insisted that Landy had the ability to speak, and they were my authorities on the subject. Under their guidance, I accepted oralism as the only right method. So I persisted, and our frustration with one another began to grow.

When Sug and I had moved to Wood River, my father had helped Sug get a job at the Alton BoxBoard, where my dad was a shift supervisor. The wages were a workingman's wages, nothing more. My father had worked there all his life, and he certainly never got rich, or even "well-off." The summer when Landy was five, however, the company's workers went on strike. Unfortunately, Sug and I had always lived paycheck to paycheck. Without his salary coming in, we were unable to pay our bills. We signed our house over to the bank, and left our friendship with Linda and Joy behind. We had no choice but to move back to my husband's hometown. Sug's sister Sue Webster and her husband Bob owned a farm, and offered to let us live rent-free in a small, empty house on their property.

Pleasant Hill was such a small community that there was no local deaf education available. We hoped the strike would end before the next school year so that we could move back to Wood River. But it was summer, school was out, and the decision for next year was still a few months away.

I set up a mirror in our country home and gathered my teaching supplies. Every day we worked on speech in front of the mirror. Feeling the sounds in the nose and the throat, Landy imitated the way my mouth formed the words. Her skills were slowly improving but I felt like something in our relationship was missing. Was I her mother or her teacher? I felt compelled to work with Landy constantly; I was exhausted, both mentally and physically. Landy often grew tired of all the voice games and closed her eyes or turned her head when she did not want to see what I was saying to her. It was so frustrating. Why couldn't she understand that we had to do this? Why didn't she understand that we had to hurry? Then she would put her sweet little hand on my face and turn it towards her so I could see what she was saying. It took a long time before Landy knew I could hear her without looking at her, but she learned quickly how to tune me out.

At the end of the summer, I met a friend for lunch at the town restaurant. A group of women was sitting a few tables away and I noticed that none of them was talking very much. One woman was not talking at all. My friend told me the woman was deaf and couldn't speak, she could only use sign language. She lived with her family on a remote farm outside of town. Apparently her family refused to learn sign language, so none of her relatives ever talked to her. Even her mother had never learned sign language. How could a mother not bother to speak to her own child? I could not get over how sad that was, my heart just broke for the loneliness the deaf woman must have felt. But maybe seeing that silent woman having lunch with her family came during the right week: the strike still hadn't ended and it was time to decide where to send Landy to school for the coming year.

The Illinois School for the Deaf in Jacksonville was the nearest school with a program for Landy. Although the residential school also had a day program, two round trips a day would have been impossible. Our hearts were breaking with the pain of having to send our daughter away to school. I remembered from the two-week seminar I had attended that the school separated the children by language aptitude. Some were taught orally, while others were considered poor candidates for oralism and were taught using sign language. To our horror, the school had just begun educating all students through a program called "total communication." Total communication means doing whatever you have to do to communicate, even if it means standing on your head. The method combines speech and speechreading with sign language. We wanted desperately for Landy to talk, perhaps not like other hearing kids, but to at least have some sort of speech. Although total communication meant she would learn sign language, the school assured us that speech would continue to be encouraged and Landy would be able to speak. So we made the decision to send her away Monday through Friday and bring her home every weekend.

I was inconsolable, but friends and family alike kept saying it was "for the best." The child's best? The parents'? I did not agree with them then, nor do I now, but I grew to accept what had to be. When the school sent long lists of all the clothes she would need, I busied myself by sewing her name on everything, right down to her socks. The school could do her laundry, but I chose to bring it home on weekends and do it myself. The chore represented another way for me to maintain my rights, my hold, as a mother.

On the big day in late August, the three of us drove up to the school. As I write this I am startled to remember that we didn't even tell Landy what was happening. We had no language for it. That one remembrance breaks my heart more than anything else, that we just walked away and she never knew where we went.

We had dinner at her favorite restaurant, McDonald's, and this became a Sunday ritual when we drove her back to the school. Landy and the other five-year-olds were going to live in the infant dormitory. It was very cute and colorful, all built to size for the tiny residents. Landy shared a room with three other little girls and I could see they would be fast friends. Because they lived together and depended on one another, as the kids growing up in those dorms did, they quickly formed their own "family." From time to time we still run across news of these girls, even though we now live in Texas. My daughter has great fun when she occasionally has a chance to see them at social functions, and later fills me in with stories of what they are doing now. I am always surprised to know that they are no longer the children I remember.

To help the kids get adjusted to being away from home, the school didn't let parents visit their children for the first two weeks. However, the school offered a beginner sign language class and we were strongly urged to attend. The school also had books on sign language we could buy, so of course we bought our own book and both signed up for the classes as well. I wasn't thrilled about having Landy use sign language, but I did want to see what she was being exposed to. After getting Landy settled in her room, we were told that the dorm's "housemothers" would get the kids busy and that it was a good time for us to leave. I don't know how Landy reacted when she realized her Mommy and Daddy were gone, but my husband and I cried all the way home. I envisioned Landy panicked, trying to find us; maybe she would think she was lost. It was a fear I would re-live many times over the years.

I believe that leaving my five-year-old daughter at a residential school was the most traumatic event I experienced as a result of her deafness. I have heard all the reasons and excuses for sending deaf children to a residential school— better education, being with "their own kind," the amount of language they can absorb, and the freedom to express themselves in their own language. Still, I feel that nothing can replace the child growing up at home if a child's family provides quality support and the public school system makes educating deaf children a priority. Years later I found out that Landy held the same beliefs. Thankfully, federal laws were passed in 1975 requiring public school systems to provide education for students with disabilities, so deaf children don't have to leave home to attend a special school. But in 1972, my life revolved around waiting for Fridays and dreading Sundays. I felt that I was a weekend mother—that this beautiful child I wanted to share my life with was being denied me.

Sug and I were living in a farmhouse surrounded by acres of land, and the nearest neighbors were at least a mile away. I had no phone, and unless I drove my husband to work, no car. My marriage was a wreck and my daughter was away at school. On Fridays I was jubilant. But on Sundays, after we went to McDonald's and I left her at the school, I cried during the drive home. The isolation led to symptoms of depression and I often slept through the week rather than face the days without Landy. I began to see a psychologist, but that didn't help me find any answers to my problems. After several months, his best advice to me was: "You know what you need to do. Until you do it, there's nothing I can do to help you." I suppose I knew divorce was inevitable, but I put it out of my mind. Instead I just tried to get through the days without the one person who loved me as much as I loved her, my daughter.

The school's sign language classes were held on Wednesday evenings. Unfortunately, the drive up to the school took an hour. The quiet of the car practically required conversation, but it had become very hard for Sug and me to be together for that long. We had signed up with every intention of completing the class, but we might have stopped going right after that first class. That evening, however, we were allowed to sneak a peek at our daughter.

Landy was walking by in a disorganized line of schoolchildren. Sug and I stood on a landing on the stairs above so she wouldn't see us. The kids were coming back to their dorm from somewhere on campus, and they all looked happy as they passed below us. The youngest was only three years old! How I wanted to run and hold my daughter, to hold all of them. We went back the next week hoping to have the same opportunity. After the second class, the tension in our marriage was just too much and we decided to study on our own. We told the instructor that winter was coming and explained that so many round trips were too much of an expense. While true, they were both still excuses.

The two weeks passed and we finally could pick her up for the weekend. I drove to Jacksonville about nine o'clock that morning and wandered the town until afternoon. I drove by the school every so often, just waiting for the time when I could have my baby back. To me, the campus looked like the world and I was in a prison that kept me locked away from my daughter. Finally, losing my patience with the clock, I entered the school.

To my delight, I was a welcomed visitor. The receptionist invited me to go into my daughter's classroom. Landy was thrilled to see me and, surprisingly, the other children were just as excited. All of the children greeted me with hugs even though they didn't know me—all that mattered was that I was a mother. Parents were popular visitors with the little ones at the school and all the kids scrambled to get their hugs. I quickly became known as "Landy's Mom," and I still wear the name today like a badge of honor. Answering her phone, I always tell the caller, "this is Alandra's Mom." The typical response makes me chuckle to myself: "Oh hi, Alandra's Mom." Some might say that I lost my identity to my daughter. I haven't lost my own identity—I've found it.

The teacher got everyone's attention again and all her students went back to their seats to show off all they had been learning. I was drawn in, mesmerized by the butterfly-like movements of their tiny fingers. Their animated little bodies seemed to be exploding with energy and emotion. To my wonderment they were reading, talking in sentences, having real conversations. I wondered how they could accomplish so much in so short a time. Then I realized that these dancing fingers were really language—not my language, but their own special language which opened all the doors that had been closed to them before.

My fears about sign language disappeared the moment I entered Landy's classroom. I still wanted my daughter to talk, but my resistance to sign language ended. It was then that I developed my love/hate relationship with the school. I missed Landy terribly during the week, but at the same time I realized a great love for her silent language and began a life-long struggle to learn it.

On the weekends when Landy was home, I did her laundry and talked to her any way I could. What surprised me most about these conversations were the *things* that she talked about. Many of them were experiences we had shared before she had the language to talk about them. All those memories had been locked just beyond my reach behind the door that said "Oral Only." Each week, Landy taught me new signs and I tried so hard to remember them until our next visit. I felt a deep sense of loss for all the early communication we had been denied because of our strictly oral approach. I missed the "baby talk" I had never heard. It would be many years before I found out that when you can see baby talk as well as hear it, it is all the more precious to the listener.

CHAPTER SIX

Stuttering with My Hands

The residential school did everything possible to keep the lines of communication open between the parents and their children. The teachers helped the children write letters home—I still have many and cherish them the same as I did the day I received them—and encouraged them to read their parents' letters aloud during class. The housemothers filled us in on health issues and clothing needs, and so our lives took on a kind of routine.

On occasion, the school hosted meetings followed by a social time for everyone to mingle and talk. There were always many deaf adults at these meetings. Because the school was in Jacksonville, a large Deaf community had grown within the town, and the deaf love to socialize. I was terrified during these events. I feared my signing was so poor that the deaf adults would lose patience with me. I could have learned so much if only I had tried to talk with them; talking to a deaf adult may have helped prepare me for raising Landy. But I always left quickly to keep the Deaf people from trying to speak to me.

Landy moved to the big dorms when she turned six. There was one dorm for girls and another for boys. There were three or four girls living in each strictly functional room. All the younger girls were at one end of the hall. The older girls were at the other end, and they shared the showers in the middle of the hall. Each end of the hall had a big TV room where the girls spent their down time. There were two housemothers on each floor, one for the older girls and one for the younger girls. To avoid having to physically wake each girl every morning, the housemothers just blinked the hall lights off and on until the girls were awake and getting ready for breakfast and school.

Landy had been living in the big dorms for a year when her housemother told me she had a story she wanted me to hear. One night that past week, the girls just wouldn't go to sleep because they were too full of chatter. Landy went down to the housemothers' lounge and reported that the girls were talking so much that she couldn't get to sleep. I thought this was really a delightful story, since all she had to do was shut her eyes. Much later I learned the truth behind this story, and it hurts me to know. After lights out every night, the girls would push their beds together. In their parents' absence, they told each other stories until they all fell asleep. The girls never asked the housemothers for comfort, I suppose the girls knew that it was only a job to them. Instead, they turned to one another for the comfort they could not get from their parents.

Although the story of Landy's "noisy" roommates has always been one of my favorite memories of her childhood, I resent the fact that someone else was there in my place to witness it. Yet what if the housemother had been thoughtless and never bothered to tell me the story? Parenthood and memories by proxy. This separation was unkind to both me and my daughter. I was denied the only thing I ever wanted—to be a good, loving mother to this child. Who did she run to when she would wake during the night? Where was the safety of being pulled into Mommy's bed and warmly snuggled until she felt safe and drifted back to sleep? I hated this school. Yet I also loved it.

One of the most fascinating things about my daughter was that after she learned sign language, she began to talk in her sleep with her hands. When hearing people talk in their sleep you are rarely able to distinguish what they are saying. The same is true for Deaf people, their signs are often incomplete and unclear because they usually only make small hand signs. I often found my daughter silently signing in her sleep when I went into her bedroom at night to check on her. Watching Landy's fingers moving, growing, and becoming the hands of a woman through the years was far sweeter than hearing the mumbled words of a hearing person. Sometimes I called my husband from the other room to watch with me, but more often I selfishly shared it with no one, standing for a long time in the weak light filtering into her room.

I wondered what Landy dreamed about and how she saw the people in her dreams. One day I asked if when she dreamed, the people in her dreams used spoken words or sign language. When she told me they used both, I asked if she always understood what they were saying. Landy told me she never had a problem communicating with people in her dreams.

As a hearing mother this thought had never occurred to me before, and I was intrigued. It was as though another piece of the puzzle that was my daughter had locked into place. Landy's mind is so different from my own, and I find it fascinating to talk with her about these things. I am so grateful that she was able to share her thoughts with me. I feel a deep sense of sorrow for the parent of any child, hearing or deaf, who lacks this kind of relationship with their child.

I was very fortunate to be able to spend every weekend with my daughter. I was horrified to learn that many of her classmates only went home when school closed for the winter and summer breaks. How could any parent stand to be separated from their child for an entire school year? Just being apart for five days was almost more than I could bear. I blamed the parents for not being more sacrificing with their time off, for not sharing it with their children. Years later I wondered how I could be so judgmental. We ourselves could have made more of an effort to move to Jacksonville so that Landy could use the school's day program. The school was in the middle of the state, so driving time for some of the parents was very long. And many children chose not to go home for visits because it meant a certain amount of isolation; at home they lacked friends with whom they could communicate freely. Besides, the school held all sorts of events on the weekends. I was told not to be surprised if

Landy asked to stay at school for some of the weekends. She never did ask to stay and I am so thankful for that. Childhood is so short I did not want to give up any of the precious little time I did have with her.

One year in the fall, Landy was asked to be in a homecoming pageant for the high school students. We were thrilled of course, and the school invited us to attend. The beautiful young women, dressed in their flowing formal gowns, paraded into the gym that had been converted for the occasion. Landy looked like a little flower girl attending to them. One especially lovely girl was chosen queen of the event. I hoped Landy would be chosen queen of the same event someday.

After all the pomp and ceremony ended, I watched the teenage girls visit with their parents. They were such lovely girls, and many of their parents were there to share their celebration. I knew those parents were so proud, how could they not be delighted with such beautiful children? But I noticed that some of the girls wanted nothing to do with their parents, not even looking at them if they did not have to. When I mentioned this to my daughter's teacher, she said that some parents didn't sign and their children retaliated by shunning them. The teacher matter-of-factly explained that it was not an uncommon reaction. I vowed to renew my efforts to learn my daughter's language.

No matter how much I practiced my signing, I was always lagging behind Landy. I lacked the language's fluid motions and beauty. Good-naturedly, Landy once told me I stuttered with my hands. She was not being critical when she pointed this out, we always point out things to one another that are funny or unique about our two cultures. I have to chuckle when I compare my stuttering to the Looney Tunes character Porky Pig, but it's not quite the same thing. It is more like I pause between words, and don't have fluid motion when I sign. I stutter when I am stressed or try to sign too fast, and I really do it when I am angry.

CHAPTER SEVEN

Home Signs

One night in 1975, Sug came home and told me he would give me a divorce. We often mentioned divorce during our frequent battles, but he always insisted he would never let me take Landy with me. After ten years, the only thing we had left in common was our love for our daughter. This time, though, he admitted he had found someone else. I was so relieved. I had wished to be out of our marriage, but hadn't left because I was afraid I would lose Landy. I had heard that couples with a disabled child often ended up getting divorced, but I don't think our marriage failed because of Landy's deafness. For that matter, I had stopped considering Landy disabled; in my mind she just spoke a different language.

Sug and I had married very young: I was just sixteen and he was twenty. As the blush wore off and we saw faults in our relationship we began to despise one another. The marriage endured for almost ten years, but there was rarely a happy moment. After all the battles and tears I just didn't matter very much to myself anymore. But Landy mattered, and I knew I would be okay because of my daughter.

The other thing that kept me strong during that time was friendship. During the years I lived in Pleasant Hill I developed only a few close friendships. One of the women had even known my husband all his life, yet still stood by her friendship with me. We have remained close friends for over thirty years. With the support of a handful of very supportive friends, I began to believe in myself for the first time in my life. The divorce was final the summer Landy was eight.

I took Landy back to my parents' home in Wood River. I was terribly frightened of the future and my parents did all they could to help us. Landy had always been very loving to her grandparents, and she enjoyed living with them. Even before the divorce, she often wrote them letters from school. She always addressed her grandparents very formally as Grandmother and Grandfather when she was small, shortening them to GM and GP as she got older.

Landy and I lived upstairs in the part of the house that had been my sister Lisa's and my bedrooms. My old bedroom became our bedroom and Lisa's room became our living area. We set up our table and chairs in one of the alcoves by the window and shared the same bathroom my sister and I had shared. We had everything we needed except cooking facilities, so we took our meals with my mother and father in the kitchen. Though Landy missed her father, a new closeness developed between us.

I knew I had no means to support a child by myself and was desperate to find a career that would make us financially secure. So while my mother watched Landy, I worked and went back to school. After getting my GED, I received a grant to enroll in Lewis and Clark Community College, where I worked towards an Associate's degree in law enforcement. I was able to get into a work-study program, and found a day job on campus in the information booth. It worked out well because I was able to study while waiting for people to come up and ask me questions.

I worked (studied) all day, then my classes started about six in the evening. I finished about nine each night. Several nights a week and on weekends I waitressed at a neighborhood bar. The bar had a grill and developed a nice family trade. It really was a nice little restaurant; but after the families went home, it was still a bar. I didn't plan on making a career out of it, I needed more for myself and my daughter.

Sug sent one hundred dollars every month for child support. But he decided he didn't want me to have custody of Landy. I still think it was just another way for him to harass me. Every six months I received a new set of legal papers. My lawyer cost six hundred dollars every time I went to court, and the stress was overwhelming. When the court battles were over, I ended up with sole custody. Sug had visitation rights every other weekend and rotating holidays. A few years later, I gave up the claim to child support (against the judge's protest) and never had to go back to court again.

My parents knew little or no sign language, so they communicated with Landy through speechreading, written notes, and "home signs." A home sign is a sign that is made up by a family member to represent an item, an action, or a need. Typically, the hearing person mimes or acts out the word with the deaf person, until they reach an understanding.

This then becomes the sign that is used between those two individuals. The same sign would have no meaning to another deaf person.

My mother was quite creative at making up home signs, and my daughter giggled when she showed some of them to me. Since many of the signs my mother made up were quite graphic, I will save her some embarrassment and explain no further. But the two of them communicated as best as they could and rarely needed my intervention.

My father was great with short notes. When I got home from work or school, it was always interesting to try to decipher his and Landy's conversations. Today, some of their most amusing notes are tucked safely away with other mementos of my daughter's childhood. My father collected stamps and he would sit for hours at his desk, which was littered with stamps and Landy's notes. Daddy often said, "If the doctors ever get an operation to fix Landy's ears, I'll sell my stamps to help pay for it." So he worked on his collection and planned for the day.

It was 1975, and Robert Redford was a great heartthrob. Landy had begun to notice boys and thought he was wonderful. I agreed—he was gorgeous. When I came home from school one day my mother was just about beside herself with laughter. She informed me that Landy had decided to write a letter to Mr. Redford. In the letter Landy told him that her mother loved him. She advised him to divorce his wife (she added that his wife was mean to their children) so he could marry her mother. Landy then insisted on a stamp, which my father, working on his collection, promptly gave her.

When Landy put the letter in the mailbox, my mother figured she would go out and retrieve it when her granddaughter wasn't looking. Well, Mom got busy during the day and forgot the letter. When she finally remembered, the mail was already gone. I appreciated the help from my matchmaking daughter and we're still waiting for Mr. Redford's response. Anyway, there was always a surprise when I came home.

One day I came home from school to find that my mother and Landy had been through an ugly disagreement. The result was a big bruise on my mother's arm where Landy had hit her. Mother displayed the bruise as though I had to see proof of the battle. Daddy had settled everyone down and for the moment they were off in their own corners. Judging from my mother's self-righteous attitude, she was just waiting for the bell. I went to tell Landy that I had heard from Grandfather that there had been a problem. I asked her to come to the kitchen so we could all have a talk.

My parents sat quietly as I talked to Landy. I soon realized that there were too many sets of house rules and they were all different. My mother had been terribly inconsistent with her rules when I was a child and I remembered how difficult that had been. My mother could give Landy love, but I was not about to let her set her rules. It was not my mother's place to make up her own rules, especially if they were different from my own. Plus, my mother had not learned any sign language beyond the basics signs for "yes" and "no"—how could she communicate right and wrong? I insisted, and my father agreed that Landy's rules needed to come from her parents even though we had separate households.

So as Landy and I discussed the problems, I wrote a set of rules and told her that both she and Grandmother would have to live by them. There would be far less confusion in Landy's life if she understood what her mother wanted and expected of her. After writing a set of "do's" and "don'ts," I posted them on the refrigerator. Signing to Landy, I said, "These are your rules, it is your responsibility to follow them. If you ask Grandmother to do something that is listed as OK on your list of rules, she has to let you do it. If it is listed as NOT OK, then don't even ask permission. Do you understand?" She signed in answer, "Yes, I understand." My parents would often chuckle about seeing her stand in front of the refrigerator checking that list before asking their permission for something. The list worked wonders, mostly for my mother, but Landy was really a very easy child to work with.

That list of rules ended the discipline problems but brought to light a new problem. A language barrier was developing in the very family that was supposed to be nurturing Landy. The problem included Grandmother and Grandfather, and also Landy's cousins, aunts, and uncles. There were some exceptions, but they were far too few. All too often I heard the request, "tell her," from family members and friends. The other common phrase was, "What did she say?"

Landy tried to follow conversations by speechreading, but in large groups that was almost impossible. Landy is actually an exceptional speechreader, and she really didn't mind if a person didn't understand sign language. But she did mind if people wouldn't even make the effort to communicate by writing. Landy had been taught Signed English, so she had learned English grammar and her writing skills were pretty good. Yet rather than even making the effort to write a note, most people relied on me to interpret. Although I did not mind interpreting for Landy, I resented having to interpret for a hearing person. If they wanted to communicate with Landy, why didn't they make more of an effort? It seemed like they were choosing the easy way out.

It became worse as Landy grew older. Family members gradually stopped asking me what Landy had said and pretended they understood her by nodding and smiling. She did speak very well, but not perfectly, and we thought they were trying to reinforce her efforts to speak. The family members who used this ruse got away with it for many years, but it became obvious that they did not understand and the lie became a source of great irritation to both me and Landy.

I began making up reasons to avoid family get-togethers. I didn't like the way Landy seemed to be left out of their festivities. I probably should have told them the truth: we actually preferred not to come. Although it would be some time yet before she acknowledged feeling left out at family gatherings, I could see her resentment growing. The saddest thing was that the family members all thought she was a wonderful child, but they would never really know her. Landy was funny and intelligent, but they hardly ever saw that side of her. In their minds they thought of her as "Tressa's daughter Landy, she's deaf, you know, but she does really well."

We loved Sue Webster's family all the more dearly because they managed to overcome the communication barriers. We had lived on their farm in Pleasant Hill, and still had a very close relationship. Six of the seven children were girls, and all of them were around Landy's age. Landy loved to spend the night—there was always something going on, from riding horses to baking bread. Sue and the kids had learned a lot of sign language, so communication wasn't a problem. Sue had the patience of a saint. When I worried about Landy being in the way, she always laughed and answered, "What's one more?" So Landy was involved in everything they did. Landy rode on tractors, fed the hogs and cows, and helped with the chores. The girls shared secrets and love, and all the things that should be a normal part of a child's life—yet they *are* missing unless there's a shared language. This part of the family was such a positive influence in Landy's life, and it was their willingness to learn and use sign language that made all the difference. Divorce is very hard on everyone in a family, but even after many years and many miles, I miss them greatly.

CHAPTER EIGHT

A Difficult Undertaking

When I took Landy back to school that fall, it felt strange to be doing so as a single mother. I would now be driving to the school from a different direction and traveling seventy miles one way. Although there was a program for hearing impaired students in our town, it was designed to fit the needs of a child who was hard of hearing, rather than deaf; and besides, it was an oral program. Landy's attendance there was out of the question. As we moved her things back into the dorm room, I reflected on the differences between the hearing and Deaf worlds. For Landy, when the doors of the school opened, they opened into her world. When I finished helping her arrange all her things just so and got in my car to drive back home, those same doors closed my daughter away from me.

During the summer, Landy had frequently written letters telling her friends of her parents' divorce. Now the girls gathered in tight little groups, gossiping about this and that, and Landy filled in the gaps about our own summer. Their conversation was mostly about the divorce. Landy now numbered among the many children who came from broken homes.

I now had to alternate weekends with her father. The time between Landy's visits was very long, and I filled the time with college courses, working, and dating. I filled the time without my daughter in the worst possible way that a person suffering from depression could: I tried to make time race, and brooded without my daughter's brightness surrounding me. Once again depression intruded into my life. I was still in my twenties, and tried to make the time pass faster by partying with my date or friends until all hours of the night. Plus, these late nights gave me a good excuse for missing work and classes. Being drunk or asleep allowed me to pass time without dwelling on my solitude. Every week I skipped more than one important class or missed days of work. I even canceled dates to stay in bed and sleep.

The weekends when Landy was home was the only time I was happy, but depression is not something one just turns on and off. When it was my weekend, Fridays were a pretty good day because I knew I would pick Landy up that afternoon. Saturdays were great, and Sundays were bad. After arriving back home from the school, the cycle of drinking and sleeping would resume.

Sometimes during my weekends with Landy, a friend would invite us to lunch or a movie. One particular weekend, Terry Crawford asked us join him for lunch. We had been good friends in high school, but had lost contact over the years. I was enjoying the opportunity to get to know him again. Terry had always been a great tease and as he started to tell me one of his new jokes I stopped him, warning that Landy was a very good speechreader and would probably repeat anything she heard to her grandparents. Landy wisely smirked at this. So not knowing a bit of sign language, Terry looked straight at her and told her if she repeated anything he said he would tape her fingers shut. Landy and I looked at each other and burst out laughing. Both of us had a wonderful time that day. I appreciated the casual way Terry accepted my daughter's hearing loss. The world of the hearing could learn a good lesson from my friend.

Terry was on the Wood River police force, and he often took his dinner break at our house. Leaning against the refrigerator, he would entertain us with his current story. His casual acceptance of Landy's deafness became one of my permanent criteria for evaluating friendships. If people appear in the least uncomfortable about the deaf, I have nothing to do with them. Acceptance also became a major consideration in choosing a husband.

The first day of classes at the community college was always the busiest, and the information desk where I worked was located in the center of the school's main hall. I was directing some new students to their classes when a guy who was an older student, probably a Vietnam veteran, walked up to my counter saying he wanted some information—but what he wanted was my name and phone number. I thought to myself, Oh brother! This is just what I need! We bantered back and forth for a minute. I didn't give him my phone number but he did learn that my name was Tressa Van Hoy (I was attending school under my maiden name) before hurrying off to class. He must have talked to someone about me, because later he stopped by to ask if I was related to Dr.

Van Hoy, who was then a dean. I said "Yes, he's my uncle," and again brushed him off. But Tom made a habit of stopping by my desk, and I began to look forward to seeing him.

Over the semester we became the sort of friends who chat casually between classes. He asked me out on several occasions and I turned him down on as many occasions. We had long conversations about topics ranging from politics to religion. Sometimes it was just the two of us, sometimes professors would join in when they had free time. When he realized I had little interest in politics (Jimmy Carter was running for President) he encouraged me to become active, and to learn which of the two parties my beliefs were in sync with. I liked the way he listened to my point of view without ridiculing or discounting what I had to say because I was a woman. My uncle, who I admired, was that type of man; but women were certainly not equal in the households I lived in. My father and my ex-husband held the firm opinion that females were the lesser sex. Being married meant that a man could have two votes, not one. I began to admire Tom for his liberal attitudes and eventually I decided that perhaps I would like to go out with him. By this time he had stopped asking. But it was the 1970s after all, so I called him up and invited him to take my daughter and myself out for an early evening. Thankfully he wasn't offended by my brash actions and accepted my invitation.

When Tom picked us up that evening, I introduced him to Landy using sign language. Later he told me I should have told him that my daughter was deaf so he could have been prepared. I truly had just never thought about it. To me, the deafness had become an incidental part of our life. I just thought he knew about her deafness from our many conversations. Thinking back to their meeting, I was impressed that he talked to Landy so naturally and didn't seemed the least bit surprised.

During the months we dated, I began to affirm my independence and voice my opinions. I just knew that at some point I would shake his liberal beliefs enough so that the "real" Tom would come out and try to assert his influence over my daughter and me. But Tom never tried to tell us what to do; he just wanted to be there for us and participate in our lives. He is a very quiet man, always taking a "wait and see" attitude. He is far more patient with life than I am. Tom was the balancing force in my life and I loved that about him. I stopped drinking, and I stopped feeling so depressed when Landy was gone. I fell in love the first time he put his arms around me; that was when I found out my car was dying. That's very traumatic when you are a single woman.

On Landy's weekends, the three of us spent our time together. We drove her back to school together on Sundays, and we talked constantly. Sometimes I signed for him, but usually he wrote notes. He also learned fingerspelling and some basic signs. Tom and I talked about getting married— there was never a beginning to our plans, we just agreed to do it. When we told Landy she readily agreed to the idea. We wanted to get married on her birthday, May 2, but the place we had decided on was booked so we had to wait until

May 6. Landy was excited, I was nervous. Tom never had much time to prepare for his new life with us. A few months after we began dating and nine months after we met, he became my husband and a stepfather to a ten-year-old girl who was already facing puberty. It would be a difficult undertaking for us all.

Tom and Landy loved each other, but his communication skills were mostly limited to fingerspelling and a barrier eventually rose between them. Throughout the early years of our marriage, though, they talked as well as they could. Tom tried to broaden Landy's vocabulary by purposefully using a word he knew she did not understand. He would slowly spell out the definition and then use the word in a sentence to further demonstrate its meaning. When he was sure she understood, they continued the conversation. Landy paid strict attention, soaking up the new words like a sponge. It was a slow, painful process but we had both been told that a lot of deaf adults graduated high school with a fifth-grade reading level.

Deaf programs do a great job teaching preschoolers to read through word recognition. When the kids get a few years older, though, it seems like the schools suddenly stop teaching vocabulary and language usage. Even though language begins in the home, we send our children to school to learn and ultimately do better than their parents. I think schools need to push, cram if necessary, language skills into all children. When we as parents lack knowledge on a subject, we hope the schools will fill that gap with our children. If educators were to take a good hard look at the current system and its less-than-perfect results, I'm sure they would see that the solution is to teach language and reading throughout the grades. If gaining our youth's interest means throwing *Moby Dick* out of the English classes and replacing it with contemporary novels, then let's do it. Without language skills a child, hearing or deaf, is disadvantaged throughout life. Yet our public schools continue to teach to a test, and that doesn't appear to be working.

Tom and I took on the challenge of correcting that problem with Landy. It was almost a game, each of us reporting to the other the new words we had given her that day. We were both avid readers and believed that if she could read and understand proper language usage, she could do anything. At every parent-teacher meeting, the teachers would ask what goals we wanted to emphasize. We always answered, "More reading and more language." During her high school years, it became a struggle to get her educators to agree to our requests. They felt Landy read well enough and would benefit more from some technical training. Tom and I continued to insist on the reading skills and in the end the educators went along with our requests. Today Landy reads on a college level and her sentence structure is almost perfect. If I could ever say we did something totally right while raising our daughter, I guess that would have to be the one thing.

Nevertheless, Landy stormed into the house one day after high school. When I asked her what the problem was, she responded, "Why in the world would the school try to teach a deaf kid poetry?" Well, maybe we had carried the insistence on more language input a little far. Still, today when speaking to a parent with a young deaf child, I tell them about the importance of improving communication—not through speech, but through the development of language and reading skills.

CHAPTER NINE

Our "Normal" Life

Six months after our marriage, Tom found a job with a transportation company that maintained a hub in Kansas City, his hometown. He had worked at various companies over the years as a transportation manager; although he hated the work, the pay was good. So we decided to move to Kansas.

There was a residential school with a day program in a neighboring city, and the local public schools also offered lots of support for deaf students. After visiting both school programs, we decided to enroll her in the public school system. The program seemed strong, they encouraged total communication, and—best of all—Landy was able to live at home. I was in heaven. This was the perfect life I had always envisioned for raising my family. Tom promised us both that we would never again live in a town that did not have acceptable education for Landy. She would never have to go away to school again. It was a promise he always kept.

Landy formed a lasting friendship with her fifth grade teacher and was an excellent student, making straight As and Bs on every report card. She even took cello lessons for a while because the teacher thought it would be a good experience for her. Even though she couldn't hear the sounds, she could feel the vibrations in the cello. Once the novelty wore off though, she wasn't much interested.

While looking through the Sunday paper one day, Tom saw an advertisement for a one-year-old Doberman Pinscher for sale for fifty dollars. After talking it over, we decided to take a look at her. We didn't tell Landy where we were going and she was thrilled when we came home with Duchess. It was love at first sight! She and Landy became inseparable and my daughter often told us, "Duch is like a sister to me."

Although Tom had been in the transportation industry in one form or another since he left the military, he really didn't like it. He decided he wanted to try to get into another line of work and began looking at the local career market. He found a new job and started training to be a store manager for a retail company. I had started a job in the jewelry department of the local Macy's and was always scheduled to work a couple of nights each week.

Our shifts were murder, and occasionally we both had to work the same night. On those afternoons, Landy came home to her "babysitter," her devoted (and very protective) pal Duchess, with instructions to lock the doors and do her homework until we got home. In case of an accident she was to get help from our neighbor, a nurse who was usually home in the evening. Landy was very responsible and Duchess was keeping her company, but I was still nervous and jumpy when I knew she was home alone.

Landy had my direct phone number at work in case of emergencies. (TTYs and the telephone relay system were still things of the future.) I instructed Landy that if she needed me, to call and just talk into the phone and I would come right home. Several months passed and things were going very smoothly. I began to relax, slipping from my normal state of tense readiness.

Early one evening while working in the department store, I got the call I had been dreading. Picking up the phone, I heard Landy talking away on the other end of the line. My legs turned weak and I started shaking from the inside out. Although I always understood everything my daughter said when we were in the same room (even with my back turned), I was lost whenever she tried talking to me over the phone. I couldn't make out anything she said and immediately feared the worst. I told my supervisor and was out the door in a flash, running all the way to the car. I blamed myself all the way home: I should have a job that would allow me to be there when she got home from school. If she was hurt, how could I ever forgive myself?

We did not live far from the store, so in just minutes I was dashing into the house. Landy sat at the kitchen table doing her homework, the ever-vigilant Duchess right at her feet. I asked Landy what was wrong and she said "nothing," looking at me as though I had just lost my mind. Even Duchess seemed to think I was crazy. I stood there puzzled, feeling foolish. I was at a total loss to make sense of the situation. I asked her, "Why did you call me at work?" She replied, "I wanted to know what time you were getting off work so I called to ask you."

My shaking legs wouldn't hold me any longer so I sank thankfully into the nearest kitchen chair. "Honey, why did you do that?" I asked. "You know you can't hear me answer you." I often forgot Landy couldn't hear. I can't tell you how many times I yelled or talked when her back was turned, but this time I think that she herself forgot she was deaf. In so many ways, deaf kids just don't realize their limitations until they are pointed out to them. My first realization of this fact came with Landy's answer. Looking a little shocked, she said, "I didn't think of that Mom, I just wanted to know—so I called."

It was true the deafness had become very unimportant to us, but this incident renewed my over-protective instincts. Naturally, after that I wanted a real babysitter for my daughter. But any time Landy needed an ally against Mother and her list of rules she almost always found one in Tom, and they both insisted that she needed to be self-reliant. If it were up to me, they pointed out, Landy wouldn't be allowed to walk two blocks to the neighborhood Quick Trip alone. I thought to myself, "At least I'm no longer introducing her up and down the street to all the neighbors so they know she's deaf." And I had long ago stopped making her wear the medical alert tag inscribed "I Am Deaf." I thought I had made great strides. In the end they won and Landy always proved worthy of the trust we put in her.

The next year, just as school was letting out for the summer, Tom got the promotion he worked so hard for. He was made manager of a new home improvement store in Orlando, Florida. We were all very excited about the move, but we were in Florida only three months when he got a second promotion to the company's home office in Fort Worth, Texas. So Landy began her next school year in Fort Worth.

We were pleased with Landy's new school. The public school system's deaf program was headed by Bill Moffat. He was loud and friendly, and the kids all loved him. Bill got to know each parent and each child; he listened to what each had to say. He had been very successful with mainstreaming deaf children into hearing classes. There were only a dozen or so kids in the program with her, and they seemed like a bright, intelligent group. Most had been in the program since they had started school. We were most impressed by Bill's dedication to serving the deaf children whose education he had been entrusted with.

Landy, who was now twelve and quite grown up, wanted to have a talk with us just before starting school. Since no one in her new school knew her by the name Landy, she wanted to leave her baby name behind, along with what she felt was her childhood. Landy was an endearing name, we told her. But she thought Alandra sounded so much more sophisticated. We accepted her request and tried very hard never to call her Landy again. Try as we might, on occasion we slipped and called her Landy in front of her friends. This was met at first with confusion, and her friends would ask, "Who's Landy?" When the pet name was explained, their confusion was followed by laughter and good-hearted embarrassment from the very "grown up" Alandra.

I always admired Alandra's ability to make friends easily with both hearing and deaf kids. Her speech was easy to understand and many of her hearing friends learned sign language very well. This was a very fortunate asset because during the summer months Alandra was mostly cut off from her deaf friends. Tom and I had not thought to get involved with the deaf society and they did not seek us out; it's a problem that still exists. Part of the problem was that the deaf kids from her school were bused in from all over the city. Because of my long work hours, I was usually not available to take her to meet with her school friends, and they were all still too young to drive themselves. So she made friends with hearing kids from our neighborhood. Our home often had extra kids visiting and Alandra visited their homes as often as she was allowed.

I was offered a manager position in a J.C. Penney's jewelry department, and accepted the job even though it meant difficult hours. Fortunately, the state's "blue law" meant that all retail stores in Texas were closed on Sundays. It was wonderful to have a full day at home with my family, and I always wanted Alandra to be home for dinner on Sundays. She was allowed to bring friends if she wanted, so we were often joined by an extra kid or two (usually a hearing kid, but they always knew sign language). Tom taught Alandra how to cook during Sunday afternoons—everything from baking bread to boning a chicken—as the two of them made dinner for whoever would be there. We even found a timer on a cord that she wore around her neck so she would know without being told when the time was up on her various dishes. Cooking was a common ground for Tom and Alandra because it was more a "doing" exercise than a "communicating" exercise. They could come together in our kitchen and enjoy one another's company without the entanglement of conversation.

We got Alandra her first teletypewriter (TTY) around this time, leasing it from the phone company. Not many of her friends had one yet, so to learn how to use it she called people she didn't really know. I don't even know how she was able to find a list of names, probably through Fort Worth's deaf support center. She was a very resourceful child.

TTYs are pretty simple to operate. They can even be hooked up so that when the phone rings, the room light will flash. TTYs look like a large accountant's calculator, except the keyboard looks more like a typewriter or computer keyboard. There's even a long digital screen that shows everything you type. Instead of figures, however, the machine shows the actual transcript of your conversation. The conversation even prints out in case the other person types too fast. Behind the small roll of printer paper is a rubber cradle. To use a TTY, you first wedge the phone's receiver into the cradle. After you dial a number, a small light blinks as the phone rings. When the light stays on, the phone has been answered. If you are calling a number where a hearing person might answer, you tap any key several times; the soft beeps let the person know they are receiving a TTY call. When you receive a TTY call, you type a greeting followed by GA, which means go ahead, and when you're ready to hang up you type SK. Rarely does anyone bother with punctuation. The conversation prints out as you go, and your words appear in lower case while the other party's words print out in upper case. An example would be:

hello ga
HIYA MOM ITS ME ALANDRA IM GOING TO BE LATE
4 DINNER GA

ok but hurry home as soon as you can ga

OK I LOVE YOU BYE BYE SKSK OR GA

ok hon I love you too bye bye sksk

The TTY was a link to Alandra's world. She spent hours on the phone, the same as any other teenager. We only had one phone line, and the soft sound of keys tapping like rapid gunfire was constantly present. I definitely recommend a second phone line to parents of deaf children. Call waiting does not work when your teenager is on the TTY—but then it probably doesn't work very well when your hearing teenager is on the phone, either. You can't lease TTYs anymore, so buy the cheapest model you can because technology is rapidly changing and improving. These days, Alandra's rechargeable TTY is the size of a checkbook, and it folds in half.

We picked up another piece of gadgetry that year that was a real miracle. It was a decoder that hooked up to the TV so that the signal could pass through the machine and print the show's dialogue at the bottom of the screen. The decoder had just come out on the market, and cost about $250. When we received a letter from school that an anonymous donor had made some of the machines available for $100, we immediately sent in our check and waited for it to arrive. The telecaptioner was a surprise, Alandra did not know we had ordered it. She was so excited when we gave it to her. We actually had to tape the movie *Blue Lagoon* twice because she wore out the first tape. She became a little disappointed because so few movies or shows were captioned, but when one came on you can bet we had to watch it. The programs that were captioned always became her favorites. Almost all new televisions these days contain decoder circuitry, so separate decoders are pretty much obsolete. Nevertheless, a dinosaur still sits atop my TV.

Despite the special equipment in our home, I lulled myself into believing that our life mirrored those of our hearing neighbors. With the exception of using sign language when speaking to Alandra, Tom and I never thought about signing to one another. Our conversations were normally about work and running the house; I didn't think Alandra would be interested. In the family I was raised in, children were not included in such conversations. She began to spend more time in her room. I had done the same when I was a teenager, so I never thought too much about it. Many years later, Alandra told me she had felt left out of my new life with Tom and that her sadness was a result of our behavior. I am sure I would not have talked to her about such mundane things even if I had still been married to her father, but it was a mistake to not sign more. Sign language was strenuous for me to keep up over long periods of time. Yet instead of practicing and making it part of my life, I neglected to hone the skills I would need for the rest of my life.

CHAPTER TEN

Half Hearing and Half Deaf?

I put a tremendous amount of pressure on Alandra to main-tain her grades. I was afraid if the deaf students in public school did not progress as well as residential school stu-dents, the government would snatch the program back and send the kids to the residential schools again. I knew it was expensive to maintain local programs for the few children attending them. However, it seemed that if public school students were successful in their academic achievements, local programs would continue to improve. Alandra remem-bered how hard it was when she woke up alone at night wanting her parents, so she worked very hard. She really liked school and filled her report cards with As and Bs. When she would occasionally bring home a C, I reminded her of her responsibility to the children coming along be-hind her. She only once said to me, "Mom, you push too hard," but she was right. Today, instead of complaining, she says, "Mother, you are very persuasive."

We had many conversations regarding her education. As I tried to help her muddle through her homework, I would say, "You will need to know this when you go to college." Sometimes tired and frustrated, she would forcefully tap her right temple with the fingertips of her right hand: "I know,

I know!" But she always brought home good grades. We always spoke with the assumption that she would one day attend Gallaudet University, never saying "if." By the time she was twelve I knew that old Dr. Bly had been very wrong about her getting a good education.

Tom and I always tried to give Alandra a hand when she had a problem understanding her homework. However, the time came when her work was beyond our comprehension. One evening she and I were struggling to understand a problem, so I said, "Alandra, you're just going to have to ask your teacher for extra help with this. Tell the teacher that you're having problems understanding." The next day I asked if her teacher had given her any extra help. Making a face, she replied, "No, she told me that she didn't have time."

I was dumbfounded. "Teachers' salaries are paid by our tax dollars," I explained to my daughter. "In other words, we pay for her to have a job. When you go to school tomorrow, tell the teacher that if she does not *have* the time, she should *make* the time. It is her responsibility to educate the children in her classes; that's what we pay her for." I asked her, "How can we parents expect our children to take responsibility for their grades, if educators will not take extra steps when our children need help?" I also reminded her that if you insist that other people live up to their obligations, you must also meet your own obligations. Her obligation was to reward the helpful teachers by getting good grades. So it was in this manner that Alandra learned to stand up for herself. Through seeking the best for my daughter, I myself had learned that many people will only give you as much as they think will satisfy you. Sometimes you have to tell them you are not satisfied before they will dig a little deeper and give you the help you expect.

Alandra and two of her friends, Tracy Mueller and Alicia McCallum, got the opportunity to be extras in a "made for TV" movie. It was one of those things where someone knew someone, who knew somebody, but it was a rare opportunity for our middle-school kids. Tom and I both were eager for her to have the experience. Because of my work schedule I was unable to take Alandra to the shoot location, so Tom took her every evening himself.

Broken Promise was partially filmed at a girl's correctional institution. It was about a pre-teen girl and her younger siblings who were abandoned by their parents during a cross-country trip. The children were split up within the foster-care system, and the story depicted their struggle to be placed in a home together. Alandra and the other girls received very small background or walk-through parts, but had a great time. After that, Alandra was bit by the acting bug. She even became pen pals with the star of the movie, Melissa Michaelson. Alandra was determined that she, too, would become an actress. A friend in the display department where I worked made a big silver star for Alandra's bedroom door—she thought that was the greatest.

I was worried, though, because I hoped she would become a teacher of the deaf or something with real stability. I felt my role was to encourage her to make a career choice that would make her a respected part of the community. Hollywood brought to mind gossip columns and career uncertainty. I certainly never anticipated that a little deaf girl could become a movie star. I now recognize that hearing parents of deaf children often place these limitations on their children whether they realize it or not. *We're* the ones with narrow views of what qualifies as "normal." As far as I was concerned, an acting career was out of the question. My own experience was that hard work, not luck or dreams, got you where you needed to be in life. Realistic or not, everyone should have a dream. How could I know what Alandra could achieve? I criticized my own parents for not encouraging my own aspirations, and here I was discouraging Alandra's dreams at every turn.

One Sunday when Alandra was about fourteen years old, she saw an ad in the newspaper for a company who was in Dallas doing screen tests. For the small sum of $150, you could film a screen test that was then supposed to be shown to all the big Hollywood movie producers. Showing me the ad, Alandra begged for the chance to do it. As usual, my skeptical answer was an emphatic "NO." I was also sure that the whole thing was a farce, a rip-off scheme. When she didn't get anywhere with me, to whom did she turn but her old buddy Tom.

In his role as Alandra's stepfather Tom often left decisions like this to me, but not in this instance. He agreed to pay the fee. We had several arguments about it during the weeks before the screen test. I told him he was encouraging Alandra's childish fantasies. His quiet but firm refrain was, "well, you never know." It seemed that Tom also dreamed of wonderful things for his stepdaughter. So off we all went to Dallas for the opportunity of a lifetime. They taped her and sent her home with stars in her eyes, telling her they would be in contact. Well, you guessed it, we're still waiting.

While this company was a rip-off, what if we had looked at other companies? What if this time I had allowed Tom to take the lead? But my practical side left neither Alandra nor Tom any alternatives; it was a one-shot chance. Looking back, I know that I was not always right—but I sure thought I was.

About that same time I noticed that Alandra had not been wearing her hearing aids. The old body aid she had worn as a child had been replaced with state-of-the-art, behind-the-ear models, and she wore one on each ear. Alandra wore her hair long (in the style of the idol of the times, Farah Fawcett) so the aids were never obvious. The first time I noticed she wasn't wearing them, I asked her if there was a problem with the hearing aids. She answered, "Oh, no Mom, I'm just out of batteries, I forgot to tell you." I bought more batteries, and the hearing aids were back for a while. But it didn't take long before I noticed they were missing again. The next time I questioned Alandra about it, she told me she had just forgotten them. I waited quietly to see what was going to happen, but they still did not show up.

After several days, Alandra came into the kitchen and said, "Mom, we have to have a talk." As usual, the phrase let me know that we were going to talk about something serious. Sitting at the kitchen table, Alandra said, "Mom, I don't really want to wear my hearing aids anymore. They don't really help me that much. I'm old enough to make my own decision about this." Alandra was about fourteen, and studying her determined face I had little choice. "All right," I agreed. "We can try this if you want, it really is your decision." Seeing her look of relief, I knew I had given my daughter the right answer. Alandra had been prepared to argue with me, but I knew that no one would know better than she if the hearing aids were helpful. I also believed she had the right to become whomever she wanted. This time, my place as her mother was to support her decision. If the choice to stop wearing her hearing aids were a poor one, we would know soon enough.

I explained all this to her teachers and the school system when they approached me with complaints. Like me, they had no choice but to acquiesce. With the aid of interpreters, Alandra was being mainstreamed into hearing classes and was doing very well. I watched closely to see that there were no setbacks. Her grades continued to be very good and she never wore her hearing aids again. A few of the other kids also stopped wearing their hearing aids, although many of her friends continued to wear them and still do so as adults.

Alandra's speech continued to develop and her vocabulary broadened nicely. Our word games had been very successful, and the English language had definitely become one of her strengths. I felt a great sense of achievement, and she was

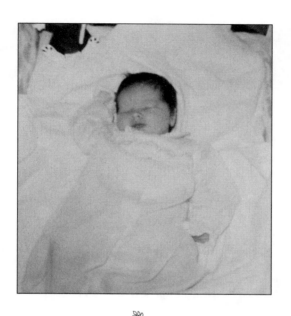

❀

From the day she came home from
the hospital, Landy became the most
important thing in my life.

❀

In the beginning, she had the support of five
generations of mothers. From left: Landy, Tressa,
Grandmother, Great-grandmother, and
Great-great Grandmother.

❀

By the time she was three, Landy was the
only thing Sug and I had in common.

❀

How could we not be proud of such a beautiful young lady?
Landy (seated, second from the right) was an attendant at the
1972 Homecoming Pageant at Illinois School for the Deaf.

❀

After my divorce, we took a
big step and started a new
family with Tom.

❀

Alandra (middle row, second from the right) began to explore
Deaf culture through Camp Sign . . .

. . . and
discovered a
passion for
acting. Here,
she is rehearsing
a scene from the
movie *Broken
Promise.*

✿

Alandra didn't have many playmates in our
neighborhood, but Duchess served double-duty
as sister and guardian.

✿

Alandra's marriage to Chad was a turning point for all of us.
Photo by Dawn Jenkins.

❀

Our wedding guests get their first taste of Deaf applause.
Photo by Dawn Jenkins.

❀

All the kids are proud to say, "Mother, Father, deaf." From left:
Chandra, Alandra, Austin, Tyler, and Chad.

proud of her skills. Alandra had overcome the language ob-
stacle; she could succeed in the hearing world. My personal
battle against the limitations of deafness was over. I was
finally able to relax, stop being the teacher, and enjoy my
child. Though I still felt as though I were leading Alandra
down the path to adulthood, I would not enjoy this smug
position for long. I was actually the one being led, towards
a greater understanding of the Deaf world and of my role in
that world.

There were so many endearing speech and language stories,
which other hearing parents of deaf children probably have
as well. I once read a quote from M.J. Bienvenu, a deaf
woman who is an interpreting instructor at Gallaudet University. She said, "Even though we don't have the sense of
hearing as our fifth sense, we have the sense of humor as
our fifth sense." This was definitely true for Alandra, who
always had such a good sense of humor about her mistakes.
The funny moments were part of her special charm. One
day, for instance, she told me that her favorite car was a
Mercedes, but she pronounced it Merkaydes. I told her it
sounded like Mer*say*dees. I had learned to read by spelling
words phonetically in order to associate them with the way
they sound. We used this simple approach to teach Alandra
pronunciation. She was like a little sponge and always remembered after having been corrected.

Another time Alandra came home from school looking
upset. I signed, "Hi Hon, what's wrong? You look down."
Alandra replied in both sign and speech, "I broke up with

my boyfriend today and he is mopping around." I smiled at the vision of the boy with a mop in his hand. I told her, "That's too bad for him, but it is pronounced moping with a long 'o'. The way you pronounced it makes it sound like he is mopping a floor because you have broken his heart." We both shared a good laugh over that, shaking her out of her sad mood.

Later that year she began pestering me for a new pair of jeans. Every Friday she said, "Mom, I need some new jeans." And I always replied, "I'm sorry, we don't have the money, I have to pay bills." After several weeks of this, I was driving Alandra home from school and she said, "Mom, I need some new jeans." I repeated my standard answer, "I'm sorry, but I have to pay bills." Alandra was a typical teenager and turned her head before I was finished because she was annoyed by my answer. Exasperated, she said, "Mom, I'm getting tired of you giving all our money to Bill. Just who is Bill anyway?" I had been fingerspelling the word bills. When Alandra turned away she missed the "s" at the end of the word, so it was no wonder she had misunderstood. I laughed and tried to explain. Tom, Alandra, and I gathered at the kitchen table that evening for an exercise in bill paying. Alandra quickly grew bored with giving our money away, but at least she understood why we didn't have the money for new jeans.

It was about this same time that we heard of a doctor in Kansas City. He was supposedly working with Dr. William

House on a new prosthesis that could create some hearing sensations in people who were profoundly deaf. Tom was originally from Kansas City and most of his family lived there, so the trip wouldn't be a problem. We talked it over with Alandra and she wanted to go. The day before the long awaited appointment, the three of us made the ten-hour drive to Tom's hometown.

The doctor told us about the prosthesis (now known as the cochlear implant) that was being developed, but was not yet successful. He performed many tests and took an x-ray of Alandra's inner ear. We learned that her auditory nerve was there, it was just not being stimulated.

Since that day so long ago in Dr. Bly's office I have tried never to allow my emotions to affect my sense of logic and understanding. That attitude has helped me maintain a rather detached clinical interest in what Alandra hears and how she hears it. Yet when the doctor asked Alandra if she wanted to hear, she asked if he could make her half hearing and half deaf. In her innocence, she said she wanted to keep both her hearing and deaf friends. The doctor thought this was a good joke. It wasn't a joke at all, and we never again discussed the possibility of an operation.

The episode in the doctor's office opened my eyes, and for the first time I realized that God must have known what He was doing. I think Alandra thought that declining an operation might hurt my feelings; I might feel as though she were rejecting not only my world, but being like me. She would be willing to have an operation, but only if it did not take her completely away from her Deaf world. Over the years I had become comfortable with Alandra being deaf. If she did not want to be hearing, I could accept that without any reservations. My religious friends and family have always told me, "In life, God gives you only what you can handle." Well, so far we had been handling the challenge of deafness fairly well. Changing our entire lives after all this time seemed a little pointless.

CHAPTER ELEVEN

Her Rightful Place

I am sure many parents would agree that the teenage years are filled with miscommunications and sometimes no communication at all. Even more problems arise when language barriers are added into the equation. Alandra and I had the normal spats typical of mothers and daughters, but usually we communicated well enough to just fight it out.

As a manager I was usually in the store ten to twelve hours a day. I rarely took a day off. At night I brought work home to study sales trends or plan for sales events. My store manager dangled a carrot, reminding me that I wanted to be considered for a corporate position when the company relocated its headquarters from New York to Texas. After a day of putting out one fire after another, I often found myself exhausted in the evening. During conversations with Alandra I began to nod in reply instead of carrying on my end of the conversation. One day, gritting her teeth at me, Alandra signed, "Why don't you want to talk to me? All you do is sit there and smile and nod your head." I had unwittingly sent my daughter the signal that I did not want to talk to her. I tried to explain, but to a teenager it just doesn't matter. Today Alandra works a lot of overtime and I see her nod in response to her own children. I look at her over the top of my glasses and smile, nodding my own head profusely. Alandra laughs and says, "But they talk so much!"

Although I sign well enough to get my point across, I have never signed to my satisfaction—and certainly not to Alandra's satisfaction. When I start to sign, my mind hears the words I want to say, but I can't seem to convert the words in my mind to the pictures of sign language. My hands seem to act on their own, making incomplete or wrong signs, even when I know the right sign. Also, deaf communities in different areas often develop their own particular signs for the same word. I think of these almost as regional dialects. In Illinois, for example, you sign "nothing" with a closed hand at about chin level, and then thrust your fingers and hand outward. In Texas, the sign is made by holding both hands in the shape of an "o" and moving them left and right slightly. Another word is "farming." When Alandra was a little girl, we made the sign by holding the left arm with the elbow bent at the twelve o'clock position, rubbing the left elbow in a circular motion with the right hand. In Texas, the same word is signed by holding the left palm up (as though waiting for something to be placed on it) and using the right hand to make lines across it as though you were tilling a field. But although my signing is not perfect, I continue to sign to Alandra, her friends, and now even strangers. Alandra would only be totally satisfied if I could sign as though I were a native signer. Few parents are ever that good, although many sign much better than I do.

In the evenings her only conversation was with a quiet Tom or an exhausted mother. Where along the way had I stopped putting forth the effort to make Alandra feel wanted? We began to look for shared interests. Alandra and I cross-stitched a tablecloth for Grandmother. Alandra had never done needlework before and she was a quick learner—

her stitches were tiny and perfect, much nicer than my own. It was a quiet time. The three of us shared a great love for books and read many of the same ones, but Tom and Alandra were never able to share much of the experience because of their inability to communicate. The two had an equal love for cooking and it was really their only common ground.

Tom signed poorly and still relied mostly on finger-spelling. He is also quiet by nature, or as Alandra says, "very boring." Tom loves Alandra, but he is not very good at expressing that love. So during many of the evenings they spent alone Alandra felt as though he were ignoring her. Alandra felt left out and lonely, and since she was an only child it was that much worse. It seemed a huge wall was coming between them. Although she still turned to him for help, later she would resent even needing him as a father figure. Also, Tom's and my ideas of discipline had reversed since the beginning of our marriage. I believed teens needed freedom and Tom thought they needed to be controlled. I thought he was being a protective father and Alandra saw him as an evil stepfather. Each felt I was on the other's side. In fact, I was trying to keep two people who loved each other from tearing each other apart; no matter what Alandra said, I knew she wanted a father.

I had to file lawsuits on several occasions when her biological father failed to send her back at the end of a visit. Once, Sug kept her all summer long (the visit was supposed to last six weeks) while I begged my lawyers in Illinois to set a court date so I could come and get my daughter. A few days before we were to go to court, he re-enrolled her in the Illinois School for the Deaf. The day before the court date, Tom and I drove to Illinois. We passed right through Wood River and went straight to the school to pick her up.

The school had a letter from Sug stating that I could not remove her from school premises, and they tried to keep me from taking Alandra. But with custody papers in hand, I told the superintendent that Sug had violated the custody order by keeping her after his visitation was over. I further warned him that they did not want to become part of my legal suit when I went to court the next day. I had made up my mind; nothing was going to stop me from taking my daughter with me.

After that, I decided I would rather be held in contempt of court than send my daughter back for any more visitations. Sug moved to Kansas that winter, while we lived in Texas and the courts of Illinois controlled the custody proceedings. I knew if Sug refused to send her back that I might spend years in court trying to get her home. Divorce can be so hard on children, they are the ones in the middle.

When I told Alandra of my decision, she was angry and tried to take the blame for her father. She told me it was her fault, because when Sug asked her if she wanted to go home to Texas, she felt sorry for him and said no. Besides, she said, it would be okay for her to spend a few years with her father since until that time she had lived with me. It was difficult for her to understand that the courts had a reason for giving custody to me rather than to her father. As far as I was concerned, there were no options; I was not about to lose my daughter. I tried to explain how much it cost every time I had to go to court to get her back, but the only thing Alandra knew for certain was that her loyalties were being torn apart.

Tom was an innocent bystander in most of the custody problems. But if there were blame to be had, regarding communication, I would put it on Tom's shoulders. He had the ability to learn sign at least as well as I, but Alandra would never hear. Speechreading is too limiting with teen-agers. Fingerspelling and writing notes are too slow, especially when tempers are flaring and heads are butting. As deaf children become teenagers, it is essential to communicate with them in the language *they* are comfortable with. Interestingly, Alandra and many of her deaf friends tell me that all deaf children wish that they had deaf parents. The deaf child thinks this would be "neat." Imagine that, what we would change in them they would also change in us. Deaf children also find their parents a major disappointment if the parents can't sign as well as Deaf people. They still love their parents, but communication is never easy. I know my mediocre sign language skills have been a disappointment to my daughter and her friends. My signing may not limit my relationship with my daughter, but it certainly limits my friendships within her circle of friends. Because the Deaf community takes in a broad age range, many of Alandra's friends are deaf women my own age. My poor sign language skills keep me from communicating with them as much as I would like.

Alandra's fifteenth year was a challenge for all of us. I noticed one week that she seemed depressed and preoccupied. When the cloud did not seem to lift after a few days, I asked her what the problem was. She confided that some of her deaf friends had told her that she was too involved with the hearing world. It seemed you are either hearing or deaf, and she needed to make a choice between the two worlds. I was crushed. My views of the Deaf world had changed drastically over the past few years, but I thought she was way too young for her peers to ask her to make that choice.

Over these many years that I have been allowed to observe and sometimes participate in the Deaf world, I have grown to think of Deaf people as their own cultural group. In fact, people who are culturally Deaf capitalize the word because it denotes more than just their hearing status. They are very cliquish and have their own clubs in most major cities. They are protective of their own, good people and bad. While I haven't noticed any racial prejudice, there is prejudice: It's Deaf versus hearing. It doesn't seem to matter to the Deaf world if you are black or white, gay or straight— but hearing or deaf matters very much. The person who runs from the Deaf world to the hearing world is not as trusted as the person who finds pride in their Deafness. As a cultural group, Deaf people constantly try to gain rights and acceptance, as well as maintain their individuality. I respect them greatly for this, even though to a great degree it leaves me, a hearing parent, on the outside looking in. Still, I have finally come to accept that my daughter is not the same as me and should someday take her rightful place in her own world.

Alandra is independent, strong, and confident. Although she was troubled by the choice she was being forced to make, I knew she would make up her own mind. Whatever her decision, it would be the right one for her. We didn't discuss it; it was her life and her choice. During the next few months she neglected to return phone calls from hearing friends and they were invited to our home less often. Anne Ables, a hearing friend who told us she wanted to become a sign language interpreter, was one of the few hearing people that Alandra still maintained contact with. At fifteen years old, my daughter became a Deaf woman by painfully closing the doors to her hearing friends.

It was also during that year that Alandra began to have some medical problems. She had always had regular menstrual periods, but suddenly for no reason she stopped having any at all. She had no spotting, nothing. Of course the first thing that came to my mind was pregnancy. Alandra and I were always very open with our discussions about sex and our bodies, and she assured me that she had done nothing to cause a pregnancy. Unmindful of her denials, the doctor first ran tests to rule out a pregnancy. Then he began the process of trying to find out what the problem was. We were sent to a gynecologist, Dr. Larry Sprowls. He wanted to avoid doing an invasive procedure unless necessary, and explained we would first run a lot of tests. I liked Dr. Sprowls very much, but it terrified me when he said that cancer might be a possibility. The doctor scheduled her for test after test; the uncertainty seemed to go on forever. I was terrified that God had decided all my children belonged in heaven and was now going to take my daughter away from me.

Dr. Sprowls still hadn't found an explanation after six weeks, so he scheduled her for exploratory surgery. Tom and I waited for what seemed like forever in the hospital's waiting area. I know I had been praying. When the doctor finally came out of surgery, the first thing out of his mouth was that he had found no cancer. Her ovaries were covered with cysts and he was not sure Alandra would ever be able to get pregnant. In my mind I whispered, Thanks for letting me keep this wonderful and rare person with me a while longer—she is all I care about, not any babies she might someday want to have. The doctor told us the problem could be handled with medication and regular check-ups.

Alandra had to stay in the hospital for several days, so Tom brought her TTY and television decoder from home and hooked them up right there in the hospital. We "camped out" with her, both of us staying at the hospital day and night until we could take her home. Despite all the special equipment we had in the room, and even though the nurses saw us use sign language, every day the hospital staff tried to communicate with Alandra through the intercom. It took several days and a few sharp encounters before we had them conditioned to bring her a note when they needed to communicate. The federal government later passed laws to make it easier for deaf people and their families to visit the hospital, but back then we were very much on our own. Yet as bad as this year had been, the worst was yet to come.

❦

Alandra still held fast to her dream of becoming a movie star, and I had not given up my hope that she would come to her senses and have more practical desires. For all my acceptance of the Deaf world and her Deafness, I still thought acting was an unrealistic goal. I wanted to protect her from certain failure and heartbreak. Yet as it turned out, I was the one who broke her heart.

One day as we were sharing our views of what the future held, Alandra again told me she was going to be a famous movie star and live in Hollywood. I told her, "You know I have always hoped you would go to college and become a teacher of the deaf." Alandra firmly replied, "No way, you just don't want me to become famous." I tried to reassure her of my faith in her. "I hope you will become famous," I said, "but in a more practical way." Alandra would not be pacified. She stood her ground, saying that I didn't have a good reason for not wanting her to become a movie star. I finally told her as gently as I could, "Hon, you can not, and never will, become a movie star." Alandra demanded, "Just why not? Explain yourself." Though it broke my heart I told her, "Because you are deaf, Alandra."

Bless her heart, she still did not understand what I was saying. It was then that I realized that she had no idea that her voice sounded different from a hearing person's voice. In my defense, this exchange took place before the acceptance of deafness in movies and television. Wanting me to be very specific, Alandra asked, "Why does that make any difference?" I steeled myself and said, "Your voice sounds different from a hearing person's voice. Even though I can understand everything you say, the people watching you on TV will probably not be able to."

It didn't end there. With her face set in defiance, Alandra said, "Tell me how I sound, I want to know." Because I had always helped her pronounce words, she knew I could tell her exactly how she spoke. Painfully, I described her words, her tone, and her inflections. I reassured Alandra that I could understand her, but I knew that I was only a minute part of her world. I still feel such shame from the experience of this one incident. Although Alandra still uses her lovely voice when speaking and signing to me, I am the reason she does not share her voice with other hearing people in her circle of family and friends. We haven't talked about it since; the sounds of silence can be deafening.

That spring, Alandra had just turned fifteen when she received a letter from Camp Sign. It was just opening this summer and they were inviting Alandra to come as a counselor-in-training, or CIT. Alandra would be bunking in a cabin filled with eight busy six-year-olds, and she would be in charge of those kids for two weeks. Thrilled, Alandra quickly let them know that she would love to be a CIT. Tom and I both drove her to the camp. It was located in Athens, in the region that Texans call "hill country." In all the years we had lived in Texas, we had never been to the hill country. The drive was breathtaking—every turn of the road brought a new glorious scene to view. Alandra, riding in the back seat, was very excited.

Alandra met other CITs her own age; they were all deaf, but everybody used a different type of sign language. Alandra's school taught her the Signed English method, but other schools used American Sign Language, Signing Exact English, the Morphic Sign System, and Cued Speech. Cued Speech is so hard that Alandra couldn't even show me an example of it. Yet these differences didn't stop the CITs from being able to communicate. Alandra went to camp for two summers in a row, and she was introduced to all these languages. She became very adept at reading them, but she did not use them herself. At camp the kids did the same things most kids do at camp—games, swimming, and lots and lots of talking—but for Alandra, I think learning the other sign languages was the best part.

CHAPTER TWELVE

Our Too Cool
Daughter

Alandra's sixteenth summer arrived and with it came her driver's license (long awaited by her, and much dreaded by us). I was commiserating with some co-workers who were also parents of teenagers, when they expressed their surprise that deaf people could get a license to drive. So many people still see deaf people as handicapped—though I believe very strongly that they are not. I laughed, and explained that loud music from the car radio never interferes with a deaf person's ability to see flashing lights. I also reminded them that a hearing person often can't hear a siren over the blare of the road noise and the radio, and that our eyes are not as keen as a deaf person's eyes. I told the remaining skeptics that my daughter often sees flashing lights in a mirror well before I see them. This conversation with my co-workers was the first time I noticed that I had taken on the role of enlightening hearing people about deafness.

When I was studying to get my license, the school taught me to drive both standard and automatic transmission cars. Today, schools only teach new drivers how to drive an automatic, and unfortunately our family's cars were standards. On the way home from the grocery store one day, Alandra begged me to let her drive. We changed positions and she started revving the car's engine, trying to make it go. When I drive, I listen to the engine and change gears based on what I hear. But I was at a loss for how to explain that to Alandra. After just a couple of jumps and bucks from the car, I lost my patience and made her get back in the passenger seat. She was so angry with me. When we arrived home, Alandra went to her room to sulk while I told Tom about what had happened. He went and got her, and together they left in his car. When they returned an hour later, Alandra was elated and smugly announced that she knew how to drive a stick shift. Believe me, I didn't line up to be one of her first passengers.

I asked Tom how he had accomplished this feat. He told me he put her at the bottom of a hill and told her to drive. (I thought to myself, Oh Lord, the transmission!) He then showed her how to watch the tachometer to know when she should shift. Several weeks later, Alandra took her driving test in our car. She must have paid very good attention to Tom's lessons because she got a license on her first try.

We couldn't afford to buy Alandra a car, so of course she borrowed ours. Usually she would pick up one of her best friends, Sherri Cupit and Carol Wilson. The three girls had been in school together since we moved to Fort Worth. Because of the distances between our homes, they were rarely able to do more than talk on the phone for hours. The girls were all about the same age, so acquiring their driving licenses gave them more freedom to socialize together. With that one piece of paper, the isolation was dispelled as if through magic.

Alandra called home one evening because she had run out of gas. I was at work with our second car, so Tom walked several miles to rescue her. On another occasion Alandra called because she had hit a curb and wrecked both the tire and the wheel rim. After spending some time thinking about this incident, Tom realized Alandra had been signing and trying to drive at the same time. That scared him pretty badly. Although he always cautioned Alandra not to sign and drive at the same time, he was just wasting his breath. When you get two deaf girls together, you can't keep their fingers still. Tom still worries about Alandra driving and signing, even though she now has more than ten years driving experience behind her.

We lived in Fort Worth, and Alandra began dating a deaf boy from Dallas. She had recently attended a party given by a deaf friend from Fort Worth, and this boy and one of his friends had crashed it. After hearing about these circumstances, I felt the boy's behavior was pretty rude; and after meeting him, Tom and I were both very against the relationship. We didn't really have a reason for our dislike, but sometimes you just get a feeling. Whenever she borrowed the car we told her not to go to Dallas, but that was a waste of breath too. Alandra is a very headstrong person.

She had been dating this boy for several weeks when she went to Dallas and stayed out too late. She was speeding on her way home, trying to get back before her midnight curfew, when a police officer stopped her and gave her a ticket. Alandra didn't tell us about the ticket. In the past few years, we'd had countless conversations about taking responsibility for one's actions, so she planned on doing just that. Also, considering the rule she had broken, it was no surprise that Alandra thought she would be a lot better off if she quietly took care of the ticket herself.

Shortly afterwards, she gave us some benign reason for going downtown to Fort Worth's Goodrich Center for the Deaf. The center was located in an old residential area with large old houses and overgrown trees. On the way home, Alandra had an accident a couple of blocks from the center. She ran a stop sign, which was blocked from view by one of the old trees. The officer who came out to the scene gave her a ticket anyway. Tom inspected the site and he agreed that the tree had blocked her view of both the stop sign and the oncoming traffic. The very next day, the city came out and cut down the offending tree. Alandra, thinking the ticket was unfair, went to court to fight it. Tom and I went with her, and she also arranged for an interpreter to be there.

As Tom and I were talking with the interpreter, he mentioned that this was Alandra's second time in court. After seeing our puzzled looks, he revealed that Alandra had indeed been at the Goodrich Center the day she ran the stop sign, but not for the reason she had given us. She had been arranging for a court interpreter because she was fighting a speeding ticket she received coming home from Dallas. For an interpreter to reveal information gained through the course of his or her duties is very unethical, but the damage was already done. Rather sheepishly, Alandra admitted to the first ticket. In the end, her hearing friend Anne Ables had accompanied her to court.

The judge dropped the ticket for running the stop sign. Although our insurance rates increased because this was a second ticket, we admitted to Alandra that we admired her for attempting to take care of the problem herself. Our pride, however, did not get her out of a talk when we got home. Alandra ended up grounded for the rest of her life, a punishment she received many times during her teen years.

Every town has its own strip, a popular place for the teen-agers to drive around. Our neighborhood kids spent many hours and gallons of gas driving up and down Camp Bowie Boulevard. One morning when my old 1969 Datsun Road-ster was in the shop (it was always in the shop), Tom and I got in his car to go to work. When he started the car, the radio came on blaring! The volume was turned all the way up, but the radio was playing nothing but static. I looked at Tom accusingly, thinking he had lost his mind and reverted to his teenage years.

Tom told me Alandra had borrowed the car the night before while I was at work. Well, we both started laughing, picturing our beautiful, "too cool," daughter driving down the strip in a car blaring nothing but static. When Tom and I arrived back home that evening, one of Alandra's teachers was visiting and we relayed the story. Although Alandra blushed, we all got a good laugh. Since Tom was a rock music fan we assured her that the radio station he listened to was very acceptable to any teenager; from now on she could just turn up the volume without trying to dial to the right station.

I often found myself defending my daughter's education needs. Until Alandra's senior year in high school, most of those battles were mild and usually took place during our biannual meetings with her teachers. I'm sure that parents of hearing children have similar struggles over education, but when I spoke against an injustice against my daughter I was also fighting for the deaf children who would come after her. If I could improve understanding of their diverse needs in just one area, it would be education. A hearing teacher of deaf students can be closely in tune with each deaf student's needs. However, teachers have a career to think about. Those who oversee teachers and school purse strings are the ones who lack the needed insight. I have never met a deaf member of the board of education, so I don't think the needs of deaf children can be fully met. Hearing board of education members will never fight within the system for deaf rights like a deaf person would. The best hope for our children's education lies with us, the parents.

Any student's senior year is a busy one, but it is much worse for college-bound deaf students. To verify that they qualify for government funds to help pay for college, they are subjected to the old hearing tests all over again. Amazingly, the government pays for these tests. I agree that the college funds must be justified, but these kids have spent their whole life in special classes because they are deaf. Do we really need to prove that they are indeed deaf? The whole thing seems a senseless waste. I suggest that a one-time parchment certificate, edged in gold leaf, would suffice. It could be issued by the esteemed doctor who first drops a pan behind the deaf child's back, then proclaims the child legally deaf.

To make things worse, students have to miss classes to take these tests. A letter we received from the high school principal called these "unexcused absences" and said that if she took the tests during school hours, Alandra would be in jeopardy of not graduating with her class. This was ridiculous, and I made an appointment with the principal to discuss the matter. Knowing how incensed I was, Tom chose to skip this appointment. Calmly (for me, that is) I explained that Alandra was required to take these tests to qualify for college funding. The principal leaned back in his chair as though he were the final word in the matter. He then explained that according to state law, a child couldn't graduate if they missed a certain number of days from school. That was enough! I lost it! I rose and stood over his desk, looking him straight in the eyes. "Dr. Galvan, I am here to inform you that there is life after graduating from high school. Unless you want me to go public with this ridiculous piece of bureaucratic nonsense, you will accept these tests as 'excused' absences." I walked out of his office, and never heard back from him. Alandra came home from school a few days later and told me that she would be graduating with her class. Our tax dollars were at work.

Days before Alandra's graduation, we lost a much loved and valued member of our family. Duchess, our Doberman, had become very ill during the past few months. She was only nine years old, very young for her breed. We had relied on her protection and companionship for Alandra for many years.

Alandra knew that I was taking Duchess to get her test results that day. At the vet's, I picked up the dog's fragile body and lifted her onto the examining table. Duchess felt nothing like her old self as I held her in my arms. She weighed only thirty-five pounds. When the vet told me the test results, I decided to give up the fight to save her and asked the vet to put her to sleep. I made the choice without discussing it with the family; it was an inevitable decision that would just be too hard on everyone. Later that afternoon I picked Alandra up from school to take her to one of the hearing tests. She asked me how "Duch" was doing. I hated so badly to tell her, knowing she would hate me for my decision, but I couldn't think of any way to delay the news. I said, "Alandra, I had Duchess put to sleep, she was not going to get any better." Crying, my poor brokenhearted child cried, "Why? Why?" Her voice was shrill and cracking with the pain of losing her beloved pet. It was a sad day for all of us and Alandra would not be consoled by anything we said or did.

Graduation day arrived; Alandra would say the day came "finally," and I would say "too soon." Her five years at residential school seemed to be time that had been stolen from me. Although I knew that childhood passes too quickly, I would have felt better about Alandra growing up if I could have had those years back. While I was busy preparing

Alandra for her adult life, I had neglected to prepare myself for life without her. I wanted to keep this child close to me forever. But Alandra was a child no longer, and I was not ready for the abrupt changes about to occur in our lives.

My parents had moved to Maine a few years earlier and were unable to travel to Texas for Alandra's graduation. The trip was just too far and too expensive, and Grandfather's health was beginning to fail. Tom's mother, as well as his sister Brenda and her husband Holland, joined us for the big event. Alandra's biological father also came; we didn't celebrate together, but Alandra spent time with both families.

It was a wonderful day full of events; we had dinner at one of the city's finest restaurants and then went to the ceremony. The graduating seniors were all dressed in emerald green caps and gowns—it seemed like there were hundreds of them. Tom and I picked Alandra out of the crowd, then we looked for her friends who had been close to us over the years. They all looked so wonderfully, radiantly happy. Few people will ever know the fears and concerns that their parents had felt when they were first told their child was deaf. And now here they were, successes every one. I was so proud for them. It was a very emotional moment for me, and I was thankful that I had been blessed with the opportunity to have a deaf child and to know these other children so well.

A row at a time rose from their seats and approached the stage to have their names called and receive their diplomas. When Alandra's row finally started towards the stage, Alandra threw her arm up and gave an "I Love You" sign without even looking towards us. She seemed so full of confidence, I was so proud of the young woman she had become.

The day after the ceremony, Alandra told me that she and a couple of her friends were going to drive up to Kansas for a visit with Sug. He and I had maintained what could best be described as a civil, but stormy, relationship. We spoke politely enough when Alandra was with us, but refused to even look at each other when she was not. I feared him even now, although I didn't hate him. I was not in favor of this trip, but Alandra was eighteen years old and I knew there was really no stopping her. I asked her to call me when she arrived so I would know they were safe, and wished her a good trip. The trip lasted only a few days and soon they were home with even more announcements.

Alandra and her two friends wanted to rent their own place, share expenses, and live on their own for the summer. Alandra's job at J.C. Penney's didn't pay that well, and I suspected Sug must have given her money for graduation. I was shocked, horrified, and totally against the idea. I was certainly not ready for this experience, and insisted to Alandra that she was not ready either. A few days later, they found an apartment.

The three of them backed a truck up to my house and my daughter moved out of our home. I was in complete shock. I was supposed to still have three months before she was grown up and gone from my care. I kept saying, "You can't move out," but she was eighteen and she assured me that she could. Grasping for anything to bring her to her senses, I asked about her college plans for the fall. To my relief, she told me she would still be going to college, but for the summer she would be living on her own. Gone again, and as she drove away with her belongings (and a few of my best towels) I saw the woman she had become. She was everything I had ever hoped she would be. Willful and headstrong, to be sure, but confident and independent as well. She never moved back home again and I have never gotten over missing her constant presence in my life.

Alandra and I spent time together to outfit her with the many things she needed for college. Because she lived on her own now, our visits were often strained. I had always been involved in her life, and now she was teaching me where my new place in this life was to be. I felt left out, like she had secrets from me. There were times when I got too pushy or nosy, or I gave her my opinion on a subject without being asked. I told Alandra that sometimes she was so hard-headed that I may as well try to talk to a doorknob as to try to talk to her. Alandra would just say "I don't have to listen to this, I have my own house now." Then she would storm out without saying good-bye, leaving me with my opinion in mid-sentence.

Often, after Alandra slammed the door behind her, I would try to keep my humor by continuing my conversation with the doorknob. The doorknob wasn't especially receptive to my opinion either, and I soon learned to keep my big mouth shut unless Alandra asked for my advice.

One day, requesting a talk, Alandra assured me that she loved me but that my job was done. I had given my daughter morals, values, and the responsibility for her own actions. I taught her to face adversity and to be able to function as a contributing member of a hearing society—and allowed her to largely reject the hearing in favor of the Deaf community. But Alandra reminded me that we were living in the eighties and it was time for me to catch up. "Mom, I'm grown up now, not a little girl any more," she explained. "You can't keep telling me what to do. If you try, I'll just stay away from you." She was right to do this, knowing her threat would be the only way I would ever let her go. It was in this way that she taught me my new role as a mother. In time I found my place in her life was just as important as before, but at that moment I did not like being left out. I missed having Alandra at home with us—but I missed a little girl, not the woman she was now.

CHAPTER THIRTEEN

My Own Place in the Deaf World

That fall we packed up Alandra's trunks and took her to Dallas/Fort Worth International Airport to send her off to Washington, D.C., home of Gallaudet University. I was relieved that she was actually going. I had feared that Alandra's taste of living on her own would ruin my plans for her future, but then we were at the airport hugging and kissing our good-byes. She was making the trip alone and would call us after she got settled in.

That evening as we waited for her call, the house felt so empty. I was nervous as a cat just waiting to hear that she had made the trip safely. Although Alandra had moved out three months before, there was finality to this that I had not felt before. When Alandra moved out for the summer, I consoled myself by predicting to Tom that she would be home in a month. Of course she wasn't. But now she would be gone for months and her bedroom seemed empty without her.

The phone finally rang and I was relieved to hear the beeps indicating a TTY call. I could hear the tone of disappointment in Alandra's "voice" even behind her excitement. If you get to know your callers well, you begin to pick up small nuances in their typing that become very much like a voice. It may be the speed of their typing or perhaps a slight hesitation in their responses, but I can usually pick up on Alandra's and her friends' moods over the TTY. She told me that the school was putting her in preparatory classes for the first semester. I asked why, and she said that they almost never put kids in as freshmen but started them off in preparatory classes.

Her best friend, Brian Barwise, had always been her academic equal and he was starting at Gallaudet as a freshman. Alandra had always made good grades and was highly insulted. I told her to just relax, that I was sure the school was doing it for the best and that everything was going to work out fine. I had not been allowed to participate in any of her pre-college meetings with her Texas vocation rehabilitation counselor. He had informed me that her future education would be based on her decisions, not mine, and that she was an adult with a right to privacy. I wasn't even allowed access to any of her test scores. Evidently Alandra had been told that she might have to take preparatory classes, but had never mentioned it.

Knowing my daughter, I knew we were in for trouble. After that, when Alandra called home I listened to the increasing discontent in her voice. I was concerned, but was not invited to get involved in the problem. She was partying at night, missing classes the next day. In October, Alandra called and complained that she was bored with the classes because they were teaching her things she had already learned. She was going to quit school and come home. I asked her to speak to the counselors, but she said she had made up her mind. She felt burned out, maybe she would go back to school later. I pleaded with her to stick it out, telling her she could never get a good job without a college degree. Having had so little formal education myself, I knew it was important for her future. Being self-taught, while respectable, does not open many career doors. Alandra told me she was going to go to work for the U.S. Post Office and that she would see me for Halloween. I tried to reason with her, but she told me she had to get off the phone, so we hung up and I expressed my opinion to the phone for a while. The results were the same as when I talked to the doorknob: Alandra would not have to listen, and I could talk all I wanted.

I didn't hear from my daughter again until Halloween night. The doorbell rang and there she was. My heart was full of mixed emotions. I was so happy to see her and hug her—I also just wanted to turn her over my knee and give her a good spanking. To this day, I don't think I have ever been so angry with her. I just couldn't understand how she could give up such a wonderful opportunity. College was not some freebie; she had worked hard and earned it. Once again, however, those dreams had been my aspirations, not my daughter's.

After we got over the joy of having her home and had visited for a while, Tom and I said we would get her things from the car so she could get settled back in her room. That's when Alandra told us that she would be living in the apartment with her friends and wouldn't even be spending the night—but that she would see us again "real soon." I was so disappointed, but understood that she needed to be out on her own. I cried myself to sleep many nights after that, peeking into her room to see the child sleeping there, her fingers dancing in her sleep. But my child was gone and in her place there was a woman I had yet to know.

With the help of her Texas rehabilitation counselor, Alandra quickly landed a job with the post office. Several other deaf people worked at the same branch. Alandra liked her job and she made a good living. It's hard to give up that kind of money and I knew that college would become a remote possibility. She worked straight nights the first few years, so we didn't see nearly as much of her as we would have liked. However, the time we did have with her was usually good. After she had to move a couple of times to new apartments, each with different roommates, Alandra announced her intentions to buy her own house.

On her own, Alandra worked with a realtor who specialized in Housing and Urban Development homes, and she fell in love with a two-bedroom condominium. She signed the closing papers on her first home a few months before her twentieth birthday, and Tom and I hadn't even seen it yet. Less than two years ago, I had predicted she would be moving back home within a month and now I had to face the truth: the move out of our home was going to remain permanent.

I was growing to know and admire this young woman who had slipped unnoticed into my child's body. Alandra was so independent. While I had twice left my mother's home for a husband's home, she was fearlessly setting out on her own. As I stood back to watch her grow, I was pleased with what I saw. During the next few years, Alandra became more and more active in the Deaf world. She still had a few hearing friends, but spent most of her free time socializing within the Deaf communities of Dallas and Fort

Worth. Occasionally she flew off to visit friends in other states—the Deaf world is really very small, and in some ways reminds me of that little town Sug and I lived in so many years ago.

I was surprised but thrilled when she became interested in deaf theater. I had only recently learned that there was such a thing, but hadn't known there was a local deaf theater group. Alandra was in a couple of productions, and my favorite was *A Christmas Carol*. The production featured two people on stage for each character: a hearing person who voiced for the hearing people in the audience, and a deaf person who signed the same part. I loved the mirror image and the visual concept. Tom and I were very proud of Alandra that night. She played three parts: The Ghost of Christmas Past and two of the female roles. I loved watching the Ghost of Christmas Past as Alandra and the voice character swirled around the stage in their flowing white shrouds.

Many of her deaf friends came up to talk to us afterwards and I felt so nervous, my old fears of signing to deaf adults coming back to haunt me. My heart was racing, my fingers felt stiff and jerky, and I stayed as unobtrusive as possible. Tom, however, was relaxed and clearly proud. He didn't care how poorly he might be communicating, he just wanted people to know how proud he was of Alandra. I stared at his painful fingerspelling, thinking to myself, "He has no idea how tedious it is for them to watch him slowly spell out all these words." Then I noticed that not only were people paying attention, they were even enjoying talking to him. Talk about needing to be hit over the head! What was I so afraid of what? I don't know, but every hearing parent I've talked with feels the same about communicating with deaf adults.

Tom unknowingly opened my eyes that night and showed me how silly my feelings were. In fact, my daughter and her friends had become the very same deaf adults I was so afraid to talk to. I resolved then and there that if I could talk with them, I could talk with other deaf people as well. It was at this moment that I gained acceptance from her friends. I also learned that no matter how awkwardly and slowly I may sign, a deaf person will give me the courtesy of their complete attention because at least I am trying. The trick was never to pretend that I understood if I did not. Deaf teens and adults hate when hearing people pretend to understand them. It's like blowing them off.

When Alandra and her friends were small children and I didn't know the sign for something, I went to great lengths to make myself understood. The roles were now reversed and I found that her friends would go to great lengths for me, pantomiming or fingerspelling to help me understand. Even stranger still was when they asked Alandra to interpret. Our roles had indeed changed. I had long ago accepted this world for my daughter, but finally I found a place in that world for myself.

Pulling me further into this world, Alandra decided to stop using her voice. Many deaf adults do not use their voices as they sign, but it never occurred to me that Alandra would simply stop talking. When I asked her why, she shrugged and said, "Most people can't understand me anyway." I must admit to being sorry that she has made this choice. I loved to hear her talk to me, and she really did speak very well. It was a skill that was hard won by both of us. We had given up so much time during her early child-hood for something that now she casually gave up. Looking back on it, I think I used her oral skills as a crutch; having Alandra use her voice made it easy for me to limit my sign language skills. I had given my daughter the ability to com-municate—now it was my turn to learn.

CHAPTER FOURTEEN

Enter Chad . . . and Tyler

Throughout Alandra's childhood, I always told her that she couldn't marry until she was twenty-five. When she was very young I told her it was against the law for a person to get married younger than that, and it was always a joke between us. When Alandra was twenty-four she asked if she could bring home a man for us to meet.

It appeared as though she wanted both Tom and me to approve. By this time, Tom and Alandra had reached another of what Tom describes as "a plateau in their relationship." Tom says, "We climb awhile, then we level off, then we climb some more." When looking at it from the outside, I have to agree that is the way their relationship seems to progress.

Alandra had been dating a guy named Chris Spalding for a couple of years, and he played in the local deaf softball league. They were talking about getting married, but Chris made the mistake of introducing Alandra to his friend Chad, who also played on the league. Chad did all he could to gain Alandra's attention during the next few months, sending her love letters, flowers, and poetry. It's a good thing she had taken that English class that covered poetry!

Alandra eventually broke up with Chris and fell head over heels in love with Chad.

It even ended up well for Chris; a few years later, he married Alandra's best friend, Carol Wilson. The two couples often visit in one another's homes and nobody harbors old jealousies or resentments. While this may seem strange to people outside the Deaf community, a circle of deaf friends may be spread across the country and still remain a very tight group. When they meet a new person at a Deaf gathering, half the fun is trying to discover shared friends or connections through their residential schools. Even when there has been little contact over the years, deaf friendships usually endure both time and distance.

Chad Bishop lived in Richardson, Texas, with his parents and younger sister (who were all hearing). We liked him right away—he was just one of those *family*-feeling guys, clean cut and nice, exactly the kind of guy you want your daughter to bring home. He immediately fit right in. Chad has sandy blonde hair, hazel eyes, and a disarming smile. He is younger than Alandra by a full five years, but you would never have known it from his behavior—he had enough self-confidence for both of them. He came from a working family and had definitely been taught the value of a dollar. A real jock, he loved all sports, but especially baseball. He joked with me and talked sports with Tom, using a combination of voice and sign. I was surprised to learn that his speech was so impressive not because he had any residual hearing, but because his parents had insisted on speech classes. We could tell he had a good head on his shoulders.

Chad seemed comfortable, as though he was not on display. His good humor and intelligence impressed me, but I fell in love with his smile. He was just what I would have wanted my boys to be if they had lived, and he quickly became like my own son. Tom and I felt confident about putting our only child's happiness in his hands. Alandra and Chad dated through the summer and moved in together in the fall. But it wasn't until Alandra said it was time for the parents to meet that I started to realize that this was pretty serious.

Getting ready to meet Chad's family was no small task; we wanted everything to go just right. It seemed so important to Chad and Alandra that their parents get along, and I shared that sentiment. The day that Chad's family came for dinner, Tom cooked while I cleaned and kept an eye out for the ferrets. About a year before, I had become enamoured with ferrets. I know they stink, but their mischievous antics make me laugh. I had two females, Peggy and Bella. During my chores I searched for the ferrets so I could lock them in their cage during the visit. Peggy was pretty laid back for a ferret and I found her quickly. Bella was still on the loose when the doorbell rang—it was our guests, a bit earlier than we expected.

After introductions, they took a seat on the couch. Chad's mother June was sweet and a little shy; her husband Wes seemed to be her opposite. Linda was a typical teenager. As we visited, I noticed June blushing from her neck all the way up to her forehead. The more I talked, the redder she got. I had just begun to think that I had offended her in some way when I realized Bella was still on the loose.

I burst out laughing, and everyone looked at me as if I had lost my mind. Ferrets can squeeze into the tiniest places, and one of Bella's favorite tricks was to hide deep inside the couch. When I sat down, she would slide under my cushion and bump me in the behind.

I asked June to stand for a second while I removed the cushion she had been sitting on. There was Bella! I grabbed her just as she started back down into her hiding place. I thought poor June was going to faint or have a heart attack, but she just said in her proper Texas accent, "Well Ah wondered what that was. Ah kept feelin' something." Which just started me giggling again. Luckily June accepted it gracefully and over the years we have become good friends. She has promised not to take legal action against me for telling this story outside the family.

Chad and Alandra became engaged that Thanksgiving. In the months that had passed I had found nothing about Chad to dislike or criticize. I was more than happy to have him for a son. Alandra wanted a big wedding, and we had a lot of planning ahead because they wanted to get married on May 29. I told Alandra that was a wonderful day for her to get married; it had been the day my first son had been born. Very sensitive to my feelings, she said, "Oh Mom, I'm sorry, we can plan it for another day." I said, "No really, the day I lost one son will be the perfect day for you to give me another." And so the planning began, which of course gave me the opportunity to spend more time with Alandra. I was almost as happy as she was.

Alandra and Chad wanted to have their ceremony performed in sign language by a deaf minister, with reverse interpretation for the hearing guests. Many of our hearing guests had never been around so many Deaf people at one time, and some had only met Alandra or Chad one or two times before. To say this would be an enlightening experience for them would be putting it mildly.

Alandra asked Anne Ables to sign a song while it played on tape. Anne had always told us she wanted to become an interpreter, and indeed she had. Alandra asked me to choose the song, so I carefully read the words to all the popular wedding music. I selected "We've Only Just Begun" by The Carpenters because the lyrics would have meaning for Alandra and Chad when they saw them in sign language.

The ceremony began and Alandra glided down the aisle on Tom's arm. She looked so radiant. I noticed through my tears that Tom was also crying. As Alandra took her place beside Chad at the altar, he took her hand and there were tears coming from his eyes as well. It was a happy moment for us all, but I think Alandra had the only dry eyes in the church. She was absolutely beautiful.

The couple said their vows, then the first strains of The Carpenters' song began to play. Anne's graceful hands signed the words to music Alandra would never hear, but the song's true beauty was in its words. In many ways, I think the song also spoke to my relationship with my daughter.

Sharing horizons that are new to us,
Watching the signs along the way,

Talking it over just the two of us,
Working together day to day together.

And when the evening comes we smile,
So much of life ahead,
We'll find a place where there's room to grow,
And yes, we've just begun.
Paul Williams and Roger Nichols (1970).
Performed by The Carpenters

Our hearing guests got a real glimpse into the Deaf world shortly after the ceremony. Dawn Jenkins, our photographer, wanted to get a picture of the new couple entering the reception area. She stood back behind the guests to get the planned shot as the minister introduced the new couple as Mr. and Mrs. Chad Bishop. As the photographer snapped the picture, all hands between the camera and the newlyweds waved wildly in the air. When Dawn delivered the wedding photos she apologized for the shot. Alandra laughed, explaining that it is the way Deaf people applaud. Deaf applause demonstrates one of the adaptations the Deaf world has made to our hearing world, and I was pleased to have such a true picture of Deaf culture preserved for us.

The next few months were filled with changes. Chad was the son I had always hoped to have, and there was no doubt he was making Alandra very happy. Because Alandra had hated being an only child, she and Chad planned to have several children. Their first child was due in the fall, so the day after the wedding I began making a cover for the bassinet I had just bought. I dreamed of them having a beautiful baby, but because of my own misfortunes during pregnancy, I secretly harbored many fears during those long months.

Thrilled with the thought of becoming a Granny, I was delighted when Alandra asked me to be in the delivery room when the baby was born. I told her I was afraid I wouldn't be able to go through with it, and that it would be too emotional for me to see the woman I still thought of as *my* baby having a baby of her own. Alandra replied that we had shared so much together in our lives, that she wanted to share this moment with her husband *and* me. I couldn't refuse. This honor was too great and one I was sure I did not deserve.

The doctor had ordered sonograms so we knew that the child would be a boy. Chad and Alandra chose the name Chad Tyler, and planned to call him Tyler. One day during Alandra's last trimester, she began having contractions. Even though almost thirty years had passed since my own premature babies had been born, I was terrified. I went with Alandra to have another sonogram done. Several other nurses and doctors came crowding in to look at the screen that showed my untrained eyes nothing. Tyler had managed to get the umbilical cord around the back of his shoulders and, grasping it in his fist, was pulling it for all he was worth. The doctor explained that they thought babies played with the cord, but it was very unusual to actually see it happening. Alandra was sent home to bed with words of caution about the positions in which she should lay. I pictured that little guy yanking on that cord and thought to myself, "Boy, he's already being mischievous, we are going to be in big trouble with this one."

Alandra brought her medical interpreter, Betty DeVries, to many of the doctor's appointments during the pregnancy. Betty is the child of deaf parents and uses sign language as though she were deaf herself. This is a great accomplishment and is held in very high regard by the Deaf community. (But it is interesting to note that when a child is raised in a Deaf household, sign language often becomes the child's first language and English becomes their second.) During the appointments, Betty interpreted for both the doctors and for Alandra. Although I still perform this function from time to time, interpreting for my daughter is not my duty or my skill. It takes a person of very great abilities to interpret in the manner that Betty does and she is obliged by her profession to go on for hours at a time. A good interpreter has the endurance of an Olympic champion, and Betty is one who has my greatest admiration.

On October 27, 1993, Alandra went into labor to give birth to our first grandchild. Chad's parents were there in the waiting room with Tom. Chad and I, along with Betty, attended to Alandra in the delivery room. I had never been involved in an occasion that required such intense use of an interpreter. Betty not only interpreted everything the doctors and nurses said to Alandra, but she also voiced everything Alandra said to them. We certainly know the kind of things women say during a delivery and I thought she should leave some of what Alandra said out. But an interpreter's job is to repeat everything without abridging the conversation, so we all got quite an earful.

Finally, after many long hours, our grandson was born. Words are inadequate; Tyler was simply the most beautiful baby I had ever seen. He looked just like his mother when she was a baby. Holding Tyler in my arms, I was reluctant to give him up. I jokingly told Chad's mother June that I was happy to share him with her and then waved his little hand, saying, "Hi, Granny June." Finally the family convinced me to let someone else have a turn and we all passed him around and took pictures. It is in this manner that we pass our life on to the next generation. After doting and cooing for hours, we finally left Alandra and Chad alone to get to know their new son.

The following morning Alandra called me through the voice relay service. The voice relay allows the deaf person to use a TTY and the hearing person to speak, while an operator acts as a go-between. The relay service is really terrific and we had long ago given up communicating by TTY. Most of the operators that I get try to put inflection in their voice and sometimes I hear them chuckle over our conversations. Male or female, they become my daughter as I talk to them, and I am only reminded that they are not when one of them begs me to please slow down.

Very cautiously Alandra told me that Tyler had failed his test. With my heart in my throat, I asked, "what test did he fail?" Alandra replied, "Tyler failed his hearing test." My first thought was one of complete happiness. I just couldn't believe how great this was. Then I was shocked by my own response as I remembered how differently I reacted twenty-five years ago when I heard the same news about my daughter. I told Alandra this was a wonderful surprise and she said, "Are you sure, Mom?" I assured her, "I just couldn't think of better news to get." She began babbling—so excited, so obviously happy—saying the doctors did not know why, that she and Chad had not even thought about having a deaf baby, and that it was just the best surprise they could ever have.

I was thrilled at the opportunity to share the life of a deaf baby again, but this time from within the Deaf world. How interesting this would be—my analytical mind was in overdrive. "It is the hearing world that lacks the ability to communicate with the deaf," I told myself, "but in this family there will be no early communication barriers."

The movie *Mr. Holland's Opus* (1995) has a memorable scene portraying a mother's frustrated attempts to understand what her deaf child needs. What the movie-goer doesn't see is that this scene plays out every hour of every day, until mother and child can find a way to communicate. In my home it lasted until my daughter was five and we finally learned some sign language. But my grandson, on the other hand, would be surrounded by language from the very beginning.

I was overjoyed with the test results. Everything was working out perfectly for Alandra and Chad and I couldn't wait to share the news with the rest of our family. I knew many would not be as pleased as we were, but that they would soon see how wonderful it was going to be. Some accepted the news immediately with open minds and open hearts; others, with sorrow. I have learned to ignore those who are negative about these circumstances unless, after all my efforts to enlighten them, they continue to lament the unfairness of it all. Then, of course, I just tell them to go fly a kite. In my experience, many people could benefit from kite flying.

CHAPTER 15

I Finally Get to Hear Baby Talk

The "No Trespassing" signs went up the day Alandra and Chad brought Tyler home from the hospital. It was made obvious that they wanted some time just to celebrate having a deaf child, not to mention simply enjoy their new baby. Chad very possessively calls Alandra "my wife" when speaking to me. I've never been sure what he means by that, but I suspect it is partly to keep me in my place. (No matter, you can forgive a good son-in-law anything, especially when there are beautiful babies, and I am sure I need help remembering where my place is at times.) On the day of the homecoming, Chad told me that "his wife" was very tired. In other words, "Grannies are not needed today," so I stayed away with restraint. Though it was late fall in Texas, believe me when I tell you this Granny was smelling the lilacs.

The funny thing was that I never felt the need to "test" what Tyler could hear. There was little use of voice and sound within his household, so how much he could hear really didn't matter. It was such a totally different feeling than when I learned that his mother was deaf, but it just seemed natural. Deafness had become the norm, not the exception, in our family. I think that it is interesting to note when we had his hearing tested through Cook Children's

Hospital in Fort Worth we discovered that Tyler actually had a lot of usable hearing. He heard so much that often his parents were not convinced he was deaf at all. Even though I reassured Alandra many times, in the privacy of their home I'm sure they did many tests to prove to themselves that he was indeed deaf.

Alandra and Chad began the input of language through sign language only. I continued to speak while signing, if for no other reason than the fact that I am comfortable with this method. I have heard of studies in which researchers taught infant hearing children to sign. They found that infants are able to communicate faster using sign language and that later they naturally convert to oral communication. I actually saw this happen with Tyler's cousin Chip.

My niece lived nearby, and her son Chip (a hearing child) was just six months younger than Tyler. Because my father had passed away the year before, my mother had moved back to Texas. We quickly put her into action as the boys' babysitter, and the two boys had been together almost every day since Chip was born. Chip began to sign with Tyler and used the signs to communicate with his mother. By the time Chip was about one year old, they had developed a language of their own, using signs that no one recognized. When my mother stopped keeping the kids the following year, Chip stopped interacting with Tyler every day. Sometimes he still tries to sign to Tyler, but for the most part that ability seems to be gone.

Tyler signed his first word when he was eleven months

old. It was not "Mama" or "Dada"—those words actually came much later than I expected. His first word was "light." Babies love to play with light switches, and Tyler was being allowed to flip the switch to gain small motor skills. At the same time, we were signing "light" to him. You wouldn't believe how we all started cheering when those little fingers made their first sign. It truly was the most beautiful sight I have ever seen. Tyler's vocabulary increased rapidly as he started asking what things were. He would point to airplanes in the sky, and then try to repeat the sign when we showed it to him. I'm pretty certain "airplane" was his second word.

Tyler learned language quicker than any other child I have ever seen. Now that he is three, he is able to have conversations like any hearing child his age. He has even been known to "eavesdrop" on conversations between his parents, or between his parents and me, and put his two cents worth in. It is such fun to talk with him, although sometimes his baby fingers make a sign that is unrecognizable and I'm frustrated because I don't understand what he wants. But even with hearing children, the mother is very often the only person who can understand toddler babble. I have finally been given the chance to "listen" to the baby talk I had always missed so much when Alandra was growing up.

Christmas Eve, 1994, both sides of the family gathered at Chad and Alandra's new house to celebrate the holiday. Chad's parents were there along with their daughter, Linda.

My mother, sister, and niece joined us, and the grannies were preparing for a fun-filled evening watching Tyler and Chip enjoy Christmas.

After the boys had torn through their presents (with much help from the grannies), Alandra announced she had a gift for Chad that she wanted to go ahead and give him on Christmas Eve rather than waiting for Christmas Day. She handed him an envelope. Chad took it from her, looked inside, then smiled and passed the envelope to his mother. The envelope passed from hand to hand until I was the last one. I still had not caught on when finally got it passed to me. Inside the envelope was a plastic thing with a plus sign on it. I looked at it dumbly as everyone waited for my response. I hate to admit that even my mother understood the meaning, but it just didn't register with me. Finally Alandra said, "Mom, I'm pregnant!" What a thrill! No Christmas will ever be the same as that one.

Chad and Alandra told us they didn't care if the baby would be a boy or a girl. They just wondered if the baby would be deaf or hearing. Sonograms are not quite that advanced yet, so we all just had to just wait and see. It was a long nine months, with everyone holding their breath to see what we would get.

My second grandson, Austin Chance Bishop, was born August 15, 1995. This time I waited in the waiting room with Chad's parents, Tyler and Tom; Chad and Betty were in the delivery room with Alandra. We did not have to wait long to meet Austin, and what a beauty he was. His features were similar to his older brother, but Tyler had dark hair and light olive skin while Austin was blonde and fair.

It was late the following day before we learned that Austin had "failed" his hearing test. While neither Chad's mother nor I felt the pain that we had felt when our own children had been found to be deaf, we were confused. This wonderful gift had turned into an enigma: why had the babies been born deaf? I had assumed that Alandra was deaf due to my exposure to rubella. June thought Chad had lost his hearing during an illness. Surely the signs were pointing to a genetic inheritance. While no one really cared where this trait had come from, the unanswered question drove Chad and Alandra nuts with wonder.

Shortly after he came home from the hospital, Austin developed a problem with his digestion. We would feed the poor little guy one bottle of milk and he would toss up two. Alandra asked me to help her take Austin and all the baby paraphernalia to the pediatrician. Dr. Janet Boone fed him a bottle of milk to see for herself. Thankfully he was in her hands, because when he started throwing up the milk he also started choking.

Dr. Boone ran out of the room with the baby in her arms, yelling "choking, choking," and I was left to tell my daughter what had happened. We followed the doctor down the hall and found her working on our sweet little Austin. We waited in the doorway so Alandra could see what was happening. He was soon breathing again, but the pediatrician said she wanted to put him in the hospital for tests.

Chad joined us at the hospital. The doctor at the hospital first made sure Austin was taken care of, then he wanted to talk to the baby's parents about their family medical history. Alandra said she wanted the hospital to call her interpreter, because she and Chad wanted to understand very precisely what the doctor was saying. When I relayed the request, the doctor seemed to hesitate. Then he questioned the need for an interpreter, because I was there and certainly appeared to use sign language. He said that he didn't think that we would need one. Then, to demonstrate his willingness to work with the "handicapped" couple, he asked me if they could read. My daughter was incensed. Her baby had almost choked to death, and now this man was not only questioning her intelligence, but suggesting they take their leisurely time and discuss it by writing notes back and forth. How were we to have faith in the man's ability to care for our very sick baby after this?

I relay this incident only to demonstrate that even today, in the country's best hospitals, an educated medical professional can be totally ignorant about the needs of the deaf population. Further, while hospitals have TTYs for their deaf patients, the staff usually doesn't know where the machines are stored and have to track them down. After the doctor displayed his ignorance, he ducked every time he saw Chad or Alandra coming and we never saw him again.

Austin had a condition known as reflux. The doctors told us that he would outgrow the condition and there was no need for surgery. He wore a monitor all the time and had to be kept in an upright position. The vomiting was so violent, it left him weak and inactive for hours. I was terrified to be alone with him for the first year of his life. But in time he did outgrow it. Now he is never sick, and eats constantly.

CHAPTER SIXTEEN

A Normal Pair of Boys

Today as I write, our little boys are growing as all children must do. My role in my grandsons' childhood is certainly different from my role in their mother's life. I am emotionally free from all the baggage I carried around when I was "the hearing mother of a deaf child." I am able to enjoy my grandsons in the same way as any other grandmother. I firmly believe it is my job to spoil and dote on them, and I perform to the best of my ability.

The only difference between me and many other grandparents of deaf children is that I'm more informed about deafness. I occasionally implement speech therapy methods —the same methods I learned at Central Institute for the Deaf—just because I want to see their response. They are interested, but only to a point. If they want to speak, they will, but it's fine with me if they don't. They are certainly getting a good education, so I know they will have the means with which to make the choice.

Tyler started school at Snow Heights Elementary when he turned three. He looks so cute getting on the bus every morning. I often drive over in the morning so that I can put him on the bus myself. It always reminds me of helping his mother onto a bus so many years ago. The other little kids on the bus, all boys, seem pleased that we sign and talk to them. Tyler and his friends saw fit to shorten my name, which is now "Tyler's Granny B" or just the sign for "B" for short. One morning Austin insisted on walking Tyler out to the bus with me. One of the boys asked me why I signed to Austin. When I told the boys that Tyler's brother is deaf, the boy signed "Wow!" I further impressed him by signing, "Mother, Father Deaf." I just couldn't resist.

Mrs. Suzanne Nichol, the school principal, puts a tremendous amount of effort into the school and everyone adores her. She attends every function that the school hosts for its deaf students, and is genuinely interested in the success of both her hearing and her deaf students. Snow Heights has a lot of parent-teacher involvement, and the classes are small. The school offers sign language classes to the entire school, and seventy percent of the hearing kids take the classes.

Tyler's teacher is Kathy Glenn. She laid the groundwork for reading the first year Tyler was in her class. The second year, Tyler was able to recognize many words and read simple sentences. She made learning fun, and Tyler cried when he found out he had to change teachers for his third year of school.

I was so amused to find out that Kathy Glenn studied at CID more than twenty-five years ago and has actually seen the training video Alandra and I filmed. Funny, how very small the Deaf world really is and how closely its people are knit. When we discovered the connection, we laughed at my 70s hairdo and Landy's unruly, curly hair. Today, both of us agree that you can gain more ground in shorter time by using total communication rather than strict oralism. Kathy was planning to retire after Tyler started his third year, but Alandra persuaded her to stay and teach Austin.

Austin is our silent one. He seems to have very little usable hearing and I think that is why he makes very little sound even when he is playing or crying. Chad and Alandra occasionally ask me to take Austin to his early intervention class. The class trains children to listen for sound and respond when they hear something. Dianne Fisher teaches the class, and she persists in her efforts to get Austin to listen. Yet he often refuses to wear his hearing aids, even for class. When he does wear them, the batteries are often dead. Alandra and Chad can't hear the device's high-pitched whistle of alert, so they have to take the batteries out to test them. They often forget to do this—hearing aids are just not a priority in their routine. Alandra shudders as she tells me that batteries would run their lives if she let them.

Dianne is a ball of energy and is actually the head of the school district's deaf program. In 1998 she began a pilot mentoring program modeled after Utah's Sky High program. The program's goal is to ease the stress when a deaf child is born into a hearing family. Dianne partners a hearing family with a deaf mentor, who comes into their home and helps them see what living with a deaf person is like. I hope they remember to mention a deaf person will leave an exhaust fan on for days, or not hear water running in the bathroom and return to find a small flood.

The school recognizes that the goals for Tyler and Austin may not be the same as the goals for a deaf child with hearing parents. The children go to speech class, but their teachers don't force them to gain oral skills. Teaching Chad and Alandra's children oral skills would make them "different" because of their almost total involvement of the Deaf community. Instead, the boys focus on communication, language, and education. For this I am very grateful. Tyler and Austin *are* normal and I would fight for their right to maintain their deaf heritage. I am glad to know that they are growing up in the comfort of the Deaf community. They already have their place in a world that accepts them.

I find myself spending a lot of time at Snow Heights. It's interesting to see the hearing parents getting used to the Deaf community. Some of them try harder than others to learn sign language, but they've all made a good first step by sending their children to a school with a strong program for deaf students.

Among the many good moms is Debi Farquhar. This is not a mother who avoids any of the challenges with her deaf son. Her son is only three, yet she is already so accepting of Deaf culture that I know she will always be included in her son's life. While visiting the school recently, a five-year-old girl named Whitney came up to Debi holding her hands up in front of her, palms to the body. Debi knew that Whitney was clearly trying to tell her something, but didn't know what she wanted. Whitney's mother signs very well and she was determined to make herself understood. The girl looked expectantly at Debi, who signed, "I don't understand Whitney, please tell me again."

Whitney put her hands up again, palms to the body, but this time she put some insistence into the gesture and gave them a firm shake. Debi shook her head and signed, "I'm sorry Whitney, I don't understand." At this Whitney gave her quite a stern look, gave up, and went over to join Tyler and her other classmates.

The last thing Debi wanted was for the child to feel that what she was trying to communicate was unimportant. But the teacher shook her head, puzzled, when Debi showed her the sign. They both walked over to Whitney and the teacher asked Whitney about the sign. So Whitney demonstrated again: hands up, palms to the body, and gave them a shake. The teacher turned to Debi and said, "She wants you to see her nail polish."

It's easy to forget that our kids are often just being kids. Their actions are not necessarily always "deaf" or always "hearing," but usually a combination of both.

Both of my grandsons, however, quickly found ways to turn their deafness to their advantage. Their favorite trick was to catch me in what can best be described as "a deaf cross fire." One would purposefully misbehave to get the game started. The more dangerous the stunt, the better. As I grabbed a handful of one boy and start signing to him, the other boy would do something equally as bad. The whole purpose of the game was to distract me from doling out "Granny's Wrath" on either brother. The game usually lasted for quite a while because they had a fail-proof excuse: "I couldn't see you telling me to stop, Granny B, your back was turned." When I finally managed to get them both under control and lined up in front of me, I got firm and carefully signed without a stutter. Because I voice when I sign, during these episodes I was usually yelling at them, too—not that it did a bit of good. In five minutes, of course, it all started again.

Tyler was in his first school Christmas program in 1996. None of us knew what his part would be, but we were all anticipating it with great excitement. The family gathered at the boys' favorite restaurant—McDonald's, of course—for dinner before the program. We gave Tyler some money for his pocket for good luck. Looking around the table, I saw my grandsons excitedly examining their Happy Meal toys; my daughter, beautiful and radiant as ever; and my mother quietly eating her dinner. Strangely, I didn't feel any different than the deaf members of my family; only my mother was left out because she didn't know sign language. I marveled at the strange change of events that had taken place in my family. Sign language had become the norm, not the exception. We didn't mean for it to happen, it just did.

We finally arrived at the school and took our places in the audience. The show began with all the three- and four-year-old students signing a holiday song. The children had only managed about two verses of "I am a Christmas Star" when Tyler looked out and saw his family sitting in the front row. When his hands grew still, I guessed what was coming. His little hands slipped into his pockets. When his teacher finally coaxed them back out, he still couldn't sign because now he was holding his money. Alandra started signing the song, trying to get him to start again. But it was not to be. He just stood there looking at us. Just before Tyler's solo, his teacher got him to put the money back into his pocket and he approached the front of the stage, signing without hesitation. This was the first time Tyler's singing teacher had "met" Alandra, and I had to laugh when the singing teacher later told me that she finally understood why Tyler could sign so well.

I decided that I wanted to spend more time with my grandsons. I wanted to see the world through their eyes and I wanted to make a difference with them. What kind of a difference? I wasn't sure, but Alandra and Chad readily agreed to my plan. So I spent that summer as their babysitter.

What a challenge it was to keep up with my grandsons! I had introduced Tyler to the computer before he even turned two. He would have spent the whole summer on the computer if I hadn't reminded him that there were other things to do. *Isaac Asimov's Library of the Universe* CD-ROM set kept him occupied for hours. Also, some of the early video games were captioned and he loved them. It was hard to say how much he could actually read, but if a game wasn't captioned he'd ask me, "B, what they say?" Tyler is very hard to keep up with, mentally and physically.

I began taking the boys to a nearby farm for horseback riding lessons. Austin wanted to learn to jump, Tyler said he didn't—but they both looked forward to their lessons. Cheryl Kleppe, their instructor, is very patient and lets the boys go at their own pace. One of the other riders at the farm, Susan, used to be a teacher of the deaf. From some of Cheryl's comments I can tell she has been asking Susan about deafness. I'm happy to see Cheryl's interest, and the boys love it when she signs something to them.

Just as fun as watching the boys learn to ride was helping them learn to swim. The three of us went swimming almost every day. Tyler taught himself to swim, and by the end of the summer he could swim five feet underwater before coming up for air. Tyler is our serious child. He says I'm his best friend, which thrills me. I hope Austin will say the same and I hope it never changes. Austin is never afraid of anything, and I call him Demolition Man. (If I tell him that something will break, he questions, Break, fix or break, finish?) But he is a sweetie. Unlike his brother, Austin loves to cuddle and always charms us with his smile.

The boys and I often walked to the park that adjoins our property. They put sticks (arrows) down the backs of their shirts and longer sticks (swords) down their pants legs. During our travels, Tyler always took the lead and marked the path with a stick. He's the big brother, but when he hesitated to try something he talked Austin into doing it first. It was amazing to watch them communicate with one another. I can usually understand their conversations, which surprises me. But lately I've noticed that I also understand more of Alandra's conversations with Chad. I hope this means I am getting better at signing. It would be wonderful to be a fluent signer by the time my grandchildren are grown.

That Christmas, Alandra surprised us with a beautiful new baby girl. Chandra was born a month early, but she considerately waited until her brothers finished opening their Christmas presents before making her arrival. After the nurses had Alandra and the baby cleaned up and settled down, Chad came out of the room. Without saying a word, he took his two sons by the hand and led them into the room to meet their sister. What a day it had been for those two boys!

Later, as she lay in the little hospital crib, I told the nurse, "Sorry, but I'm going to clap my hands over her." The nurse nonchalantly shrugged her shoulders, but her eyes fell to the baby as I clapped my hands. Chandra lay as peaceful as could be. Smiling, I said in voice and sign, "She's a deaf baby." The nurse said, a little rudely, "That doesn't mean anything." I just replied, "You want to bet on it?" And I was right.

CHAPTER SEVENTEEN

Smelling the Lilacs

In a few weeks the new sign language class will start at school. My husband and I will be there, along with my mother, sister, and niece. Each of us has different reasons for joining the class. I want to be able to follow other people's signed conversations, and I don't want to be lost anymore when an entire group is using sign language. Tom thinks learning to sign will bridge the gap between him and his daughter and keep one from building with his grandchildren. My niece has rearranged her work schedule to attend, saying that some day Alandra and she will be alone in the family and that she wants to be able to talk to her so they can stay close. My mother still babysits for the boys and they can be very demanding when they think she should be able to understand them. She'll be happy to gain any words she can.

It seems our family members' eyes have been opened to our communication shortcomings. For some of us it was having deaf grandchildren, for others it was because they are living close to Alandra again. My writing this book may have even played a role. Whatever our reasons, everyone seems anxious to get all they can from the classes. I wish it had not taken so very long for this kind of acceptance within our family, but am grateful that it came at all.

I would give so much to be able to turn back the hands

of time so that I might have talked candidly to a deaf adult. I was always too concerned with what was proper and what might offend. As children, we are taught to be polite by not staring or asking questions—the very things that could help us understand and accept people's differences. If I could have had this conversation with a deaf adult all those years ago, and they had told me, "it will be okay," would I have had the capacity to understand? Would I have been able to see and embrace the future as I am able to now?

When I first learned that my daughter was deaf, I didn't know any Deaf people who used sign language. There certainly were no hearing people who thought it was worthwhile. These days, it seems that everybody who meets our family ends up wanting to sign. Tyler and Austin are in day care, and five of their teachers are now actually taking sign language classes. What a terrific thing for them to do! And when the boys first started horseback riding lessons, Cheryl, their instructor, knew nothing about deafness. Now, she tries to learn at least one new sign a week.

It's very fulfilling to watch my grandchildren grow up. During the boys' horseback riding lessons, Susan sometimes interprets for me so I can just stand back and watch. I hope that working with horses will teach the boys that communication doesn't necessarily mean speech or sign language, but they are practicing clucking their tongues and saying the word "Whoa" just the same.

Holding our beautiful Chandra takes me back in time. She looks so much like her mother; it is as if I am holding

Landy again. She has her mother's dark hair, but like her brothers, it will probably change to her father's sandy blonde. Alandra tells me she is finished having babies because she's a little afraid of having a hearing child. Yet the genetic counseling doctors tell us there is no chance of that happening because Alandra and Chad's matched set of genes would allow all their children to be deaf. Where that gift came from is anyone's guess.

Austin isn't as quiet as he used to be. He had to start talking so he could tattle on his older brother; Tyler wasn't about to do that kind of talking for him. (I should ask their mother to write up a list of rules for my refrigerator.) Sometimes I intervene in their battles, reminding them that being brothers is very special. Other times I let them fight it out. My grandsons, after all, are just normal little boys. But as the two of them nap, I watch their little fingers and wait.